A Daily Dose of Godly Encouragement:
Medicine for Tough Days

Book 3: Summer

Larry E Davies

Copyright 2024 by Larry E Davies
All rights reserved

ISBN / 979-8-9892756-2-5

A percentage of the income from this book series: "A Daily Dose of Godly Encouragement: Medicine for Tough Days" will be donated to Micah Ecumenical Ministries: a network of nine downtown churches in Fredericksburg, Virginia. Through Micah, the churches cultivate a continuum of compassion with unhoused neighbors. Its ministries address basic needs, health care, housing, income, and spiritual support. The organization envisions a community where all neighbors have a home.

For more information: micahfredericksburg.org

Table of Contents

Forward	v
July	1
July 1 – Surfin' for the Lord	2
July 2 – Surfin' for the Lord – Conclusions	4
July 3 – Power of The Word	7
July 4 – America	10
July 5 – Derecho	13
July 6 – Scams, Con-Artists, Jacob & God	16
July 7 – Scams, Con-Artists, Jacob and God – Conclusion	19
July 8 – Please Lord… No Meetings!	22
July 9 – Fired!	25
July 10 – God's Invitation	28
July 11 – God's Invitation & Sri Lanka	30
July 12 – Sri Lanka	32
July 13 – Michael	34
July 14 – Breaking The Peanut Butter Habit	37
July 15 – Breaking the Peanut Butter Habit – Conclusion	40
July 16 – Courage and Foolishness	42
July 17 – David and Revenge	45
July 18 – David and Revenge – Conclusion	47
July 19 – Curse of the Pink Flamingos	49
July 20 – Journey Church	52
July 21 – FreeCell	55
July 22 – Ten Questions	58

July 23 – Ten Questions - Conclusion	60
July 24 – Modern Day Disciples	63
July 25 – Flashlights & The Beatitudes	66
July 26 – Healing Service	68
July 27 – Healing Service – Conclusion	70
July 28 – A Healing Story	73
July 29 – Storms & Lighthouses	76
July 30 – Bad Day!	78
July 31 – Six Strong Men	80
August	**83**
August 1 – Preacher Stories	84
August 2 – Halftimers	86
August 3 – Half-Timers: Success to Significance	89
August 4 – Rodney	92
August 5 – Chairs	95
August 6 – Remembering Zig Ziglar	97
August 7 – Traveling	100
August 8 – A Diverse World	103
August 9 – Zulu	106
August 10 – Jerks	109
August 11 – Punishment	112
August 12 – Reaching Our Youth	115
August 13 – Clutter	118
August 14 – Clutter – Conclusion	120
August 15 – Arnold Palmer	123
August 16 – Integrity	126
August 17 – "Think of Me" Remembering David	128

August 18 – A Key Mystery	131
August 19 – Wild Weddings	134
August 20 – Suitcases & Stress	137
August 21 – Blockbuster Video	140
August 22 – Blockbuster Video and The Church	143
August 23 – Blockbuster Video & The Church – Answers	146
August 24 – Help: I Can't Control My Dog!	149
August 25 – Vital Congregation	152
August 26 – Elvis	155
August 27 – Elvis & The Interview	158
August 28 – Elvis: The Mystery Voice Revealed	161
August 29 – Hope	163
August 30 – Monkeys	166
August 31 – A Cure for Identity Crisis	169

September **172**

September 1 – Katrina And Twenty Beds	173
September 2 – Catastrophe, Hope & A Lighthouse	176
September 3 – After Katrina	178
September 4 – What's Wrong with my Parrot?	182
September 5 – Windshield or Bug?	185
September 6 – Where Are You God?	188
September 7 – Readers Give Thanks	190
September 8 – "Do It Again"	193
September 9 – Pianos, Rats and Born Again	195
September 10 – Coping with Grief: Joel Warren	198
September 11 – Ground Zero	201

September 12 – A Professor the Mideast & Depression	205
September 13 – Answers: Following God and Dealing with Depression	208
September 14 – Carl	211
September 15 – Beverly Hillbillies Go to Church	214
September 16 – Jed Clampett and Grannie Preach	217
September 17 – "I Don't Eat Pork!"	220
September 18 – Moses and Failure	223
September 19 – 1953	226
September 20 – 1953 Change, and The Church	228
September 21 – Church Response to 1953	231
September 22 – Letters	234
September 23 – Stress Disease	237
September 24 – Success	240
September 25 – Make A Difference?	243
September 26 – Computer Crash	245
September 27 – Computer Crash & Four Prescriptions	247
September 28 – Prescription #2	250
September 29 – Prescription #3	253
September 30 – Prescription #4	256
More from Larry Davies	**260**

Forward

Nothing describes summer better than visiting the beach: walking in the hot sand, surfers shootin' the tube, beach volleyball, laying on a towel sunbathing, visiting souvenir shops and listening to Beach Boys music. I grew up in Virginia Beach, Virginia and spent several summers as a teenager working and playing near the beach. As a pastor, I often thought about returning to pastor a church on the beach, but it wasn't until after I retired that I got the opportunity to serve Virginia Beach United Methodist Church.

Every day I had the opportunity to take a walk on the beach boardwalk and enjoy the atmosphere. I learned something though. There are parts of Virginia Beach that tourists don't often see. In addition to the large hotels, expensive restaurants, and beach homes there are also the working poor riding to work on bicycles from a nearby trailer park or run-down hotel and the homeless sleeping on benches along the beach.

Churches near the beach are actively providing food, shelter, medical aid and financial assistance. One member of our church owned a successful bicycle shop. When he retired, he sold the shop, but donated his tools and his inventory to our church. That owner and other retired folks now repair or provide bicycle transportation to anyone who needs it. One person had a vision from God and possessed the ability and talent to turn that vision into an awe-inspiring reality that helps thousands of people in need.

In this book as in others, you will hear stories of encouragement to face those tough days we all face from time to time. You will also hear amazing stories of people and churches accomplishing remarkable ministry. You will read stories of healing and healing services. There are miraculous mission trips to Sri Lanka after a tsunami and Mississippi following a hurricane. There are also stories about wild weddings, the Beverly Hillbillies and Elvis. Finally, there is a series that starts with a computer crash that leads to me discovering Four Prescriptions for life and a promise from God.

Paul once gave this advice to a young preacher named Timothy: "Do not waste time arguing over godless ideas and old wives' tales. Spend your time and energy in training yourself for spiritual fitness. Physical exercise has some value, but spiritual exercise is much more important, for it promises a reward in both this life and the next. This is true, and everyone should accept it." (1Timothy 4:7-9)

"A Daily Dose of Godly Encouragement: Medicine for Tough Days" represents a summation of my attempts over the past thirty years to plant God's seeds of encouragement and hope within you. This book, "Summer" represents July through September of a year-long opportunity to provide meaningful and transforming daily medicine. There have been many doses of Godly encouragement planted in my life over the years. Some of those came from within my family and friends and some from the many churches I served. I am so grateful for the people who influenced me.

My wife, Mell, stuck by my side all these years providing encouragement and love. She has faithfully been with me at every church I served.

My children, Stephen and his son, Jackson, my daughter Lisa and her husband Bobby and their son, Carson, my mother, Martha and my sister Kathy and her husband Greg have all been supportive in so many ways.

I've served many churches and they all provided inspiration and encouragement. So many people touched my life. Some appear in my stories but all of them made a difference in my life, and I am grateful for their support and love.

My prayer is for you to read and enjoy the daily doses of Godly encouragement, knowing that God wants to bless and inspire you. I pray you will use these stories as part of your devotional and prayer life and trust God to guide you from there.

I would love to hear from you. You can like one of my pages on Facebook: Larry Davies or Sowing Seeds of Faith or you can visit my website at www.SowingSeedsofFaith.org or email me at LarryDavies@PrayWithYou.org.

May God bless you richly on your faith journey.

Larry

July

July 1 - Surfin' for the Lord

Philippians 4:4-9

The 1960's and 70's for teenagers in Virginia Beach often included surfing. Surfers dared to be different. Most teens wore blue jeans, but surfers wore corduroys and T-shirts with surfer logos. We drove mom's car, but surfers drove vans. Thanks to the influence of Beach Boy's music and beach flicks, surfers were cool dudes and I wanted to be one. Looking back on my foolish quest, I discovered lessons that can help us all be more successful in life and improve our relationship with God.

First: Why use a battleship… when a surfboard will do? To surf, you need a board. Virginia Beach has small waves, so surfboards are small and lightweight. My father bought a board from a sailor out of Hawaii that was eight feet long, made of oak, weighed seven tons, and nicknamed 'the battleship.' People on the beach laughed. Surfers in the water paddled far away from me.

Lesson: Good preparation beats frettin' any day. Nike says, "Just do it!" God says, "Don't worry about anything; instead, pray about everything." (Phil. 4:6) The best preparation for living your faith is a growing relationship with God. Prayer, Bible study, small groups and worship strengthen your foundation.

A Daily Dose of Godly Encouragement: Medicine for Tough Days

Second: Are you doing too much paddlin'… and too little surfin'? Do you know how much energy it takes just to paddle to the surfing area? (Especially with a battleship.) I would huff and puff, thrashing my arms, only to have the next wave pick up the surfboard and fling me back to shore. I was too pooped to surf.

Lesson: Is your 'work at it' too large and your 'faith in it' too small? Frank Sinatra sang, "I did it my way." God says, "If you do this, you will experience God's peace, which is far more wonderful than the human mind can understand." (V 7) It's easy to get caught up in church activities and forget that church is meant to prepare us for how we involve ourselves in everyday life.

Third: A sleeping surfer… could get stung. After finally reaching the surfing area, I could rest. One time, I fell asleep, woke up, looked around and saw a huge jellyfish. So much for teenage coolness as I screamed and fell off the board setting a new speed record swimming to shore.

Lesson: Do you know when to relax and when to be alert? In this scary world, working to have a better relationship with God can set our priorities straight. Then we are more able to rest peacefully and be more alert when necessary. "Fix your thoughts on what is true and honorable and right." (Verse 8) Good preparation is so important. Strengthening your relationship with God can be a key ingredient.

Next: More lessons from Philippians and Surfing.

July 2 - Surfin' for the Lord - Conclusion

Philippians 4:4-9

My foolish venture into surfing led to discovering lessons that can help us all be more successful in life and improve our relationship with God.

Fourth: Waxing your board… beats breaking your gourd. After finally getting into position, I was ready for my first ride. I pictured hangin' five or ten. For you nonsurfer dudes, that's curling five or ten toes over the front edge of the board. The right wave arrived, and I paddled like mad to catch it and stood up. (Pause) No one told me a surfboard needed to be waxed. I was trying to stand on a 'slip n slide.' Well, I slipped and slid off the board like it was a gigantic banana peel. So much for hangin' ten.

Lesson: A willingness to prepare can save a lot of despair. "Think about things that are pure and lovely and admirable. Think about things that are excellent and worthy of praise." (Phi 4:8) Waxing your board is a necessary preparation for good surfing. Strengthening your relationship with God is a necessary preparation for good living.

Fifth: How do you… steer this thing? After applying three pounds of wax, I went out again, caught a wave, stood up and stayed up. But then I faced another problem. How do you steer this thing? Steering was critical because the surfing area was limited and extremely crowded. The 'Battleship' and me were bearing down on some poor schmuck and all I could do was shout, "LOOK OUT!" It is amazing what a moving surfboard can do. He stepped back just as my board landed and he was flipped high enough in the air to qualify for a pole vault competition. They asked me to leave the beach that day.

Lesson: A continual willingness to get up after failing is often the crucial ingredient for success. Never, never, never give up! "Keep putting into practice all you learned from me and heard from me and saw me doing." (V 9) A huge part of life is handling disappointments, obstacles, challenges, and setbacks. Our faith is seldom strengthened by our success. Faith grows stronger or weaker as we manage crisis.

Sixth: Shootin' the tube… makes a happy surfer dude!
Finally, I began to get the hang of surfing. There are few thrills that compare with catching a wave and riding it all the way to the shore. Surfing is ultimately a combination of preparation, patience, a never-give up attitude and a deep love and respect for the power of the ocean wave.

Final Lesson: Could this also be the secret of living a godly life? A combination of preparation, patience, a never-give up attitude and a deep love and respect for the power of God? Once you get the hang of it; there is no thrill to compare with totally surrendering your life to God. Nothing! "And the God of peace will be with you." V9

Prayer Challenge: What daily habit can you start or improve today?

July 3 - Power of The Word

John 1:1-18, 1 Timothy chapter 4

After two long days and nights of fruitless searching, a weary volunteer passing a wooded area for the umpteenth time spotted a tiny bare foot protruding from the underbrush. Gently, she cleared the leaves from the motionless three-year old boy. "Billy, Billy, wake up. Are you okay?" Slowly, one eye began to open, then another. "Where's my mommy?" he hoarsely whispered. Hundreds of neighbors, rescue personnel and family came running to see the most precious sight in the world. A precious child was lost, feared dead, but now he was found, hungry but alive.

What's going on? Who is Billy? Were you involved in the story? It's interesting how words can move you from laughter to tears, expose painful memories or provide the motivation to accept a new challenge. Have you ever read a story and couldn't stop? But what about God's Word? Can an ancient collection of words still change lives even now? Here is what the Bible itself says:

- Your word is a lamp for my feet and a light for my path. (Psalm 119:105)
- Every word of God proves true. (Proverbs 30:5)
- The grass withers, and the flowers fade, but the word of our God stands forever. (Isaiah 40:8)

- In the beginning the Word already existed. He was with God, and he was God. (John 1:1)
- For the word of God is full of living power. It is sharper than the sharpest knife, cutting deep into our innermost thoughts and desires. It exposes us for what we really are. (Hebrews 4:12)

A light for my path. The truth, which has always been that will stand forever. The living power that cuts deep into our innermost thoughts and desires. Can God's Word really do all that? Yes, and more. Shortly before becoming a minister, I was invited to a breakfast honoring a missionary from Uganda. She was politely thanking people and talking until she came to me. She did not know me or my future, but she paused, took my hand and looked deep into my eyes. She asked: "Are you going into the ministry?"

Startled, I replied: "Yes I am, but how did you know?"

"Never mind," she said. "What is important is God wants me to say something to you!"

I was stunned. Nervous already about my career change, I needed to hear something from God. But she didn't know me or what I was experiencing. What could she possibly say that would resolve my fear and confusion?

What she said next, I will never forget. **"God says, you are to keep your nose buried in the Bible. Your first**

priority is to teach God's Word." She then turned away. How right she was. Paul said to Timothy: "Until I get there, focus on reading the Scriptures to the church, encouraging the believers, and teaching them." (1 Timothy 4:13)

After years of fruitless wandering your weary eyes scan a passage of Scripture for the umpteenth time. Suddenly you spot a tiny nugget of truth amidst the words. A soft voice whispers, "Wake up! Are you okay?" Slowly, one eye begins to open, then another. "Come quick! A precious child was lost, feared dead but now is found, hungry but alive."

Prayer Challenge: This summer, commit to a daily Bible or Devotional reading.

July 4 – America

Psalm 8

Forbes magazine once listed 100 great things about America. A few that stood out for me were: The Declaration of Independence, The Constitution and the Bill of Rights, Baseball, Food in New Orleans, Rock and roll, iPod, iPhone, iPad, and everything Apple, Barbecue, Broadway, Mark Twain, The Super Bowl, Monopoly, M&M's, Facebook, Thanksgiving, Pickup trucks, The Simpsons, Frisbees, Harley Davidson, March Madness, and I would add with a smile, anything Taylor Swift.

July 4 is Independence Day, a time for celebration and for reflection. We celebrate who we are as Americans, and we reflect on the values that define us and the sacrifices made on our behalf. Those examples and sacrifices were evident when I visited South Korea. We were showered with kindness from the very beginning. I learned that Americans have a unique relationship with Korea. Two stops on our tour illustrate why.

First was a trip to Yanghwajin Foreign Missionary Cemetery. 145 graves belong to foreign missionaries and their families who dedicated their lives to God through service in Korea. Many gave up promising careers to live in a land unknown to westerners at the time. Korea was a hostile place for Christians.

Missionaries could not start a church or even preach in public. Penalties were severe. Yet despite the persecution and danger, the missionaries profoundly influenced Korean society, not only by establishing hospitals and schools but by affecting its intangible values, thus contributing to the abolition of the class hierarchy in old Korea. Some of those who came to Korea to spread the Gospel also shared in the sufferings and hardships.

The second visit was to Odusan Unification Observatory on the DMZ, the dividing line between North and South. This dividing line and the controversy surrounding the splitting of the country led to the Korean war. The United States played a pivotal role. Over 128,000 Americans were either killed or wounded. Thousands more Americans continue guarding the border, the DMZ. Between the observatory and North Korea is a short stretch of water. As you look through binoculars you can't help but notice the stark difference between the two countries. Across the water, there are no high-rise buildings or traffic jams, just an eerie quietness. Relations with North Korea are described as fluid or more accurately, full of ups and downs. This tension which at any moment could erupt into war is key to understanding the role of faith and prayer in the lives of many South Koreans. Today, Seoul looks and feels much like any other sophisticated city.

The pastor of our host church said, "We will always be grateful for the sacrifices made by American missionaries and later, American soldiers. We would not be the country we are today without the support of the United States." As we celebrate Independence Day, I can't help but think of the influence we continue to have on the world around us. I pray that influence will always include our trust and faith in God.

Prayer Challenge: Today, read Psalm 8 and be thankful for our many blessings.

July 5 - Derecho

Matthew 5:38-48

According to Wikipedia, "Derecho is a widespread, long-lived, straight-line windstorm associated with a fast-moving band of severe thunderstorms." I've never heard the word before and prefer to never hear or experience a "Derecho" again. If you want a story, ask virtually anyone in our area: "How long did you go without power?"

Over the first few days, I saw examples of a crisis bringing out the worst in people. There were reports of fighting over generators at hardware stores as well as long lines and arguments at gas stations. I walked into a grocery store while one of the workers was bringing out a shopping cart full of bottled water. One man grabbed the entire cart in front of the waiting crowd and callously took it to the checkout register.

But I also heard about the dedication and hard work of utility workers, city employees and volunteers who worked long hours in extreme heat under difficult and dangerous circumstances. There were pastors and churches that delivered water, offered showers, opened their buildings as cooling stations and checked up on the elderly. A wedding was held at a church with no power: hot, dark but still beautiful. A get-together was hosted by several families for their church rather than letting the food spoil.

Jesus said: "If a soldier demands you carry his gear for a mile, carry it two miles. Give to those who ask, and don't turn away from those who want to borrow." (M. 5:41-42)

Carrying two miles is beyond the norm and displays to others a "can do" spirit that stands out in a crowd. Being a follower of God is never promised to be easy. At times of crisis the road can be slippery, unclear, and treacherous. Jesus never walked an easy road. The early disciples faced a "Derecho" of difficulties, yet they continued, and lives were changed, churches formed, and ministries begun. Charles Tindley wrote: "When the storms of life are raging, stand by me. When the world is tossing me, like a ship upon the sea, thou who rules wind and water, stand by me."

Clarissa Estes wrote: "Refuse to fall down. If you cannot refuse to fall down, refuse to stay down. If you cannot refuse to stay down, lift your heart toward heaven and like a hungry beggar, ask that it be filled, and it will be filled. You may be pushed down. You may be kept from rising. But no one can keep you from lifting your heart toward heaven — only you. It is in the midst of misery that so much becomes clear."

During a "Derecho," remember the God who will always be there to stand by you. Strengthen your resolve, travel the extra mile and in the midst of crisis, lift your heart toward heaven and refuse to fall down.

Prayer Challenge: Help me Lord be someone with more of a "can do" spirit.

July 6 - Scams, Con-Artists, Jacob & God

Genesis 27:1-45

Did you ever receive an email like this? "I am former Mrs. Abibat Said, a widow to the late Alhaji Mahi Said. I am 72 years old, suffering from a bout with cancer. My late husband was very wealthy, but he died during the Gulf war. I inherited all his business and wealth. I have now decided to divide part of this wealth by contributing to the development of philanthropism in Africa, America, and Asia. I selected your organization to receive $10 Million dollars. Please immediately get in touch with my physician and business manager to file for the transfer. I await your urgent reply."

"You will receive ten million dollars?" Wow! This seems astonishing until you hear the rest of the story. People responding to the request are told to simply divulge their bank account number and a huge deposit will soon follow. What actually occurs is a huge withdrawal -- of every dollar in your account. Authorities estimate victims have lost billions. Fortunately, I was never one of those.

Not so fortunately, I became casualty to another internet scam. An order came over our Sowing Seeds Ministry website for 175 copies of one of my books with credit card information. The address was in Africa so I was suspicious. I called my local banker and asked his advice. "Have you received payment?" he asked. "Then ship it and don't worry," he said. Unfortunately for me, my banker was wrong.

Days later, I received a phone call informing me that the order was processed with a stolen credit card. Within days, all the money was withdrawn from my account. Our little ministry was successfully scammed out of thousands of dollars and 175 copies of my book are now floating around, somewhere in Africa.

When describing the first email scam, I felt smart but succumbing to the lures of the second scam made me feel embarrassed, and angry. "How could I be so stupid? Why didn't I act on my suspicions? Why would someone want to harm our ministry?"

Then there is the story of Jacob and his twin brother Esau in Genesis. Jacob was the second twin and was born holding tightly to Esau's heel. The name Jacob means, "grabber" or "deceiver." Jacob was a con artist, and one person he conned was Esau. He stole his brother's birthright with what I call, "The World's Most Expensive Stew." Caught in his deceit, Jacob did what comes natural for any con artist -- he ran away. For years he stayed with his Uncle Laban, yet another con artist in the family.

Years later, Jacob wants to pack up his family and return home. All his life, Jacob has run from trouble but now the con-artist was coming home to face Esau, his family and God. In one of the most unusual encounters in the Bible, Jacob, the con-artist faces the music and learns a valuable lesson from God about confession and forgiveness.

Next: Jacob comes home.

July 7 - Scams, Con-artists, Jacob and God - Conclusion

Genesis chapters 32-33

I described succumbing to the lures of an internet scam which made me feel embarrassed and angry. I'm beginning to understand how Jacob's brother, Esau felt. Jacob grabbed Esau's birthright. Caught in his deceit, Jacob ran away. All his life, Jacob had been running but now the con-artist was coming home to face Esau, his family and God. For years, Jacob escaped the consequences of his deceit and lies. But no more. He would soon face the truth before his brother, who was riding out to greet him – with four hundred armed men. What would they do to him? Fearful, Jacob sent his family across the river to act as shields while he stayed safely behind.

But during the night, Jacob experienced a significant turning point which changed his life forever. There is a mysterious wrestling match. Was it real? Was it a dream? Was it an angel or God? Then the mystery man said, "'Let me go, for it is dawn.' But Jacob panted, 'I will not let you go unless you bless me.' 'What is your name?' the man asked. He replied, 'Jacob.'" (Genesis 32:27) According to custom, Jacob would not ordinarily divulge his name to a stranger because it was believed to reveal your character and surrender power to the person asking. Yet, to this stranger, Jacob gives his name. He confesses that he is Jacob, the deceiver, the con artist.

Jacob needed to wrestle with the consequences of his life of lies and deceit. What happens next is one of those significant Biblical moments. "Your name will no longer be Jacob," the man told him. "It is now Israel, because you have struggled with both God and men and won." (Genesis 32:28) But what does it all mean? There is a Jacob of "grabbing and deceit" within all of us. Someday, we must face our own wrestling match with God. Recognizing who and what we are is a necessary step toward divine change. A willingness to change allows God the opportunity to work a miracle within you. Did Jacob really change? Absolutely! How do I know? Read on.

"Jacob saw Esau coming with his four hundred men. Jacob now arranged his family and went on ahead." (Genesis 33:1-3) Did you notice the change? The former con artist and coward who hid behind his family and possessions now moved ahead to face his brother – alone. But Jacob wasn't the only one who changed. Esau, the scammed brother, also experienced the miracle of change. "Esau ran to meet him and embraced him affectionately and kissed him. Both were in tears." (33:4)

The one with every right to seek revenge instead chose forgiveness. Is it any wonder that Jacob would say to Esau: "To see your friendly smile is like seeing the smile of God!" (Genesis 33:10) Such is the power of divine grace. Jacob's wrestling match led to a changed life. Esau's willingness to forgive led to the miracle of reconciliation.

Have you been scammed, taken advantage of? Are you struggling with bitterness, vowing to get even with a relative, coworker or friend? Have you scammed others? Maybe it's time for your own wrestling match with God. Confession leads to change. Change followed by reconciliation is potent medicine for the soul. Like Jacob and Esau, this could be a turning point that will change your life.

Prayer Challenge: Help me forgive those who harmed me. May others forgive me.

July 8 – Please Lord... No Meetings!

Hebrews 10:19-25

"I hate meetings!" I'm not kidding! One thing I didn't anticipate when becoming a minister was the absurd number of meetings that come with church life. Have you ever been to a board meeting with the main topic being whether to pay someone to cut the grass or use volunteers? Churches often have hundreds of committee meetings, each jam-packed with issues. For example:

- Who left the lights on in the men's bathroom last week? (Wasting money)
- Did you hear what happened to Martha last night? (Gossip)
- There's a bunch of spoiled food in the refrigerator. (Clean-up)
- Who's cooking the hot dogs after church this Sunday? (Hey... I like that one!)

Do you see the picture? It's not pretty! But after many years of ministry, I've learned an amazing truth! Are you ready? This will surprise you! The issue isn't about meetings at all. Nope! The real problem is my leadership and my bad attitude. As pastor, I was the one who needed to mend my ways.

A Daily Dose of Godly Encouragement: Medicine for Tough Days

"Without wavering, let us hold tightly to the hope we say we have, for God can be trusted to keep his promise. Think of ways to encourage one another to outbursts of love and good deeds. And let us not neglect our meeting together, as some people do, but encourage and warn each other, especially now that the day of his coming back again is drawing near." (Hebrews 10:23-25)

In other words, we gather at a meeting to hold tightly to the hope God promised. Meetings should be used to encourage one another to outbursts of love and good deeds. The idea is not to stop meetings but rather to use meetings as a source of encouragement, an opportunity for teaching and especially a divine call to action.

Now, before any meeting I ask: Is God invited? More than a perfunctory prayer or devotion, this question is a spiritual challenge. Do you want something more specific? Do you begin the meeting seeking God's direction? Do you start and finish on time? Is there a written agenda? Are you providing adequate information? Are you making reasonable decision-making progress? Is there an atmosphere encouraging creative thinking? Do you offer opportunities for friendly disagreement? Is there reasonable consensus with the direction of the group? Has the overall atmosphere been encouraging? Do you end seeking God's blessing for your action?

Now, after carefully following all the lessons learned -- I love meetings! (No I don't.) We never argue! (Yes, we do.) Our discussions are always relevant! (No, they aren't.) But we are making solid progress and God's hand is gently guiding our ministry. Just one more thing: "Who is cooking the hot dogs?"

Prayer Challenge: Lord, help me have a better attitude about meetings? Ugh!

July 9 - Fired

Romans 5:1-5

As a college student, I was promoted to a manager's position at a local restaurant. Students were not usually offered leadership positions, so this was a great opportunity. One of my duties was turning off lights at closing time by flipping a series of circuit breakers. Another manager gave me instructions, but in my nervousness, I couldn't remember what he said. So, I guessed, figuring to have someone check before leaving. In the rush, I went home, forgetting the circuit breakers.

Early the next morning, as I arrived at work, people were running in and out of the building carrying boxes of meat into a refrigerated truck. The owner called me to his office and angrily informed me that I had turned off the power to the walk-in freezer. Most of the food valued at several thousand dollars would be thrown out. I made a major mistake. No excuses would be accepted or tolerated! It was my responsibility!

I was told to resign as manager but offered an opportunity to remain as an employee. Unfortunately, my fierce pride took over my common sense. I angrily refused their offer and quit. At this point, you could focus on my mistakes (there were many) and justifiably say I deserved my fate. True. Or you could righteously proclaim I was an innocent victim of poor management procedures that allowed no margin for error. They should have put a chart on the fuse box. True again.

Both views contain an element of truth, but I needed encouragement. Having never lost a job before, I believed life for me was over. After all, what else was I good for? How would I recover? Holding a job was my identity. What would I do now?

The Apostle Paul suffered and understood what it meant to be rejected and discarded; yet he still managed to write these stirring words of encouragement and hope: "We can rejoice, when we run into problems and trials, for we know they are good for us—they help us endure. And endurance develops strength of character and character strengthens our confident expectation of salvation. And this expectation will not disappoint us. For we know how dearly God loves us, because he has given us the Holy Spirit to fill our hearts with his love." Romans 5:3-5

Looking back, I realize losing my job was difficult, but not the end of the world. There were lessons that would improve my later performance as an employee and a leader. I learned the importance of being better organized, listening carefully and asking good questions. God uses even our failures as learning tools for growth. God loves us, even when we are fired.

Ultimately everyone stumbles but the successful folks are the ones who learn to get up again and again, dust themselves off and continue their God-chosen path. For that, "We can rejoice."

Prayer Challenge: How has God encouraged you during difficult times?

July 10 - God's Invitation

Luke 14:1-24

Church leaders occasionally tell me: "There is little hope for our church to have any influence in our community much less the world. We are a small church and only getting smaller. We can hardly pay our pastor and other bills much less help anyone else. We have few young people. We can't afford additional staff. Our volunteers are faithful, but they are old and tired. What are we to do?"

Jesus said: "A man prepared a great feast and sent out many invitations. When all was ready, he sent his servant around to notify the guests that it was time for them to come. But they all began making excuses. One said he had just bought a field and wanted to inspect it. Another said he had just bought five pairs of oxen and wanted to try them out. Another had just been married, so he said he couldn't come." (14:16-20)

God is inviting us, the church, to a great feast; so great, that nothing else should take precedence. The invitations come first to guests who usually attend any great feast. The so-called 'good' people of the community, the same people who would also proudly claim membership to a church. Yet, these very people, 'good' people who receive gold embossed invitations from God are the same ones who for one reason or another are unable to attend the most important event of all time: claiming to be busy buying land or other business necessities or too busy with personal matters. Excuses! Good excuses but excuses just the same. Wait! Don't judge them too quickly.

Remember these excuses? "We are so small. We have very few young people. We have no money. Our members are old and tired." Sound familiar? God's response? "The servant returned and told his master what they said. His master was angry and said, 'Go quickly into the streets and alleys of the city and invite the poor, the crippled, the lame, and the blind.' After the servant had done this, he reported, 'there is still room for more.' So his master said, 'Go out into the country lanes and behind the hedges and urge anyone you find to come, so that the house will be full. For none of those I invited first will get even the smallest taste of what I had prepared for them.'" (14:21-24)

As the church we receive the first invitation to God's feast, but we are expected to respond. If we don't, God will invite others and we will miss out. How are we to respond when we are so limited? What does God expect us to do? Good question.

Next: God's Invitation and Answers!

July 11 - God's Invitation & Sri Lanka

2 Corinthians chapter 8

As the church we receive invitations to God's feast, and we are expected to respond. If we don't, God will invite others and we miss out. The 'feast' describes God's opportunity for us to say 'yes' to the invitation knowing that serving God is more important than our occupation, our family or even our very lives. We say yes trusting God for answers, resources, and courage. Can it be that simple? I struggled with this question. Our church was active, but we were not a mission-oriented church. Then several members traveled to Jamaica offering medical aid. Their stories and the change God brought into their lives had an impact.

The Apostle Paul wrote: "For I can testify that they gave not only what they could afford but far more." (2 Corinthians 8:3) As Christians, we are judged not by church attendance, Bible study, or the size of our offering. These aspects of our faith help us become better Christians, but we will be judged by how generously we respond to needs. True giving is a lifestyle and a ministry that involves our time, skills, and enthusiasm. Paul continues: "Since you excel in so many ways-you have so much faith, such gifted speakers, knowledge, enthusiasm, and such love for us, now I want you to excel also in this gracious ministry of giving." (8:7)

As a part of becoming more giving, our church chose to expand our giving and involvement through prayer support and volunteering within our local community and other parts of the world. That same year, a massive Tsunami swept the Indian Ocean. More than eleven countries were struck by the enormous waves with a loss of life at more than 300,000. Our church raised money. But, now what? How could we become more directly involved? As we searched for answers, God began to change our church.

We visited a local aid agency specializing in getting medical equipment and supplies to other areas where needed. Our first project involved receiving and sorting large bales of used hospital linens, boxing them to be shipped to third-world countries. The second project involved shipping 40,000 pounds of rice to a Tsunami struck village in Sri Lanka.

The CEO of the company asked me: "Would you like to go with us and see the rice for yourself, assess the damaged area and look for opportunities to help Sri Lanka in the future?" Ten days later, I secured a passport, received my shots, and began a series of flights that would last over twenty-six hours and take us half-way around the world.

Next: Sri Lanka

July 12 - Sri Lanka

James 2:14-26

God challenged our church to think bigger, and miracles followed. Can we say 'yes' with faith to God's invitation knowing that serving our Lord is more important than our occupation, our family and even our very lives? We say yes trusting God for answers, resources and courage. I fearfully said 'yes' obtained a passport and was soon on a flight with three other leaders to the other side of the world.

We flew to the tsunami-ravaged beaches of a fishing village: Kalmunai. The news reports could not prepare us for the devastation. Demolished fishing boats littered the beach. Piles of brick and rubble, scattered among palm trees, represented houses and businesses. The destruction stretched for miles along the beach and at least a mile inland. Clusters of white flags marked mass graves.

A woman approached me with a plastic bag clutched in her hands. She handed me a type-written piece of paper describing how she lost all seven of her children. Through an interpreter, she said to us, "Please pray for my family. I have lost them all." All I could do was exclaim, "I am so sorry!" and cry. At one point, we were surrounded by an angry crowd. We heard: "You come to take pictures and make promises. But you go home and give us no help."

A Daily Dose of Godly Encouragement: Medicine for Tough Days

"Suppose you see someone who needs food or clothing, and you say, 'Well, good-bye and God bless you; stay warm and eat well' — but then you don't give that person any food or clothing. What good does that do?" (James 2:15-16)

We promised the people of Kalmunai we would not abandon them. Amidst the rubble, I picked up a cluster of fishing net and showed it to several men as they described their desire to go back to work. "We must fish to survive!" they emphasized. We learned that for $3,000, a new fishing boat equipped with a motor and nets could be built locally. With each boat, four families could work and ultimately thrive.

Within days of our return, people throughout our area responded. Churches, clubs, families, and businesses adopted fishing boats. By the end of the campaign, our community purchased thirty-three boats. More importantly, a sense of hope was restored as one community aided another.

God continually sends invitations to be the church during challenging times. Our faithful response should be to say 'yes' to the invitation knowing that serving God is more important than our occupation, our family or even our very lives. We say yes trusting God for answers, resources, and courage to enable us to do far more than we ever imagined possible.

Prayer Challenge: Lord, help me accept your invitation to help those in need.

July 13 - Michael

Psalm 121

I received the following email from Michael: "I read your devotion about suicide and wanted to send you my story: How God saved me from doing it. My name is Michael. My Mother said she named me after the Archangel. I hit bottom and was suicidal. My friends were using me. I have constant pain in my back, neck, and upper body from a truck accident. I have a constant ringing in my head that keeps me awake at night. Most people seem concerned about only themselves. I thought people were going insane. I lost my jobs due to irritability and frustration. I was fed up with living."

"I prayed many times for God to use me. I wanted to be in situations where I could help others. I felt called to lessen the stress and pain suffered by so many, but I began to feel God was not listening. I lost my purpose in life and there was no reason for me to stay around. At one time, I was a dedicated part of a youth ministry. I went to Bible College. But before the end of the semester, I was kicked out for being a disruptive influence. I was asking too many questions. After that I left the church and Christianity. I was angry for the "brainwashing" by my youth group."

A Daily Dose of Godly Encouragement: Medicine for Tough Days

"I was still seeking the truth. I prayed many times for God to lead me, but I was prideful and thought I could figure out most of the truth for myself. At times it seemed I was being led back to the Christian church, but I did not want to go. I even studied witchcraft and other things. I became a Tarot card reader. I felt able to help people by reading their cards and counseling them. I was at rock bottom. But I did manage to get help and spent fifteen days at a hospital."

"After getting out, I still had suicidal feelings but decided to try working in a homeless shelter and see if I could get something going. At the shelter they have worship services with guest speakers from different churches. I began to see how God was leading me back to Him. I began reading the Bible. I discovered God has been there all the time, but I wasn't listening. I had too much pride. I was influenced by anti-Christian friends. I lost my self-respect."

"I needed to allow God to change me, and He did. There has been a major transformation in my life. I have really changed. Recently, I spoke at the homeless shelter, and many told me the message really touched them. I found a church to become a part of and I am on the road to a life serving Christ. And to think, I prayed for God to take my life. I guess He did, but not in the way I intended. I feel loved and secure thanks to almighty God. Thank you for listening." -- Michael

Are you considering suicide? Please think again! There are other options. Michael certainly discovered a better option. The 988 Lifeline provides free and confidential support for people in distress 24/7.

Prayer Challenge: Help me be more aware of the emotional needs around me.

July 14 - Breaking The Peanut Butter Habit

John 4:1-42

My son, Stephen, loved peanut butter sandwiches. Love is too mild. He -- LOVED peanut butter sandwiches. Every meal, he wanted a peanut butter sandwich: not a peanut butter sandwich with jelly; just peanut butter. We traveled to restaurants carrying a paper bag that always contained a peanut butter sandwich. Sigh!

Stephen was also very stubborn. Especially when it came to his eating habits. When he set his little mind to something, it was like trying to stop a freight train. "Would you like a hot dog? Spaghetti? Broccoli?"

"No! No! No!!!" You could see his look of determination and tears. "I want my peanut butter sandwich!!"

As a parent, I simply could not let this continue. Something had to be done! (I know better now, but Stephen was my first child. I hadn't read the training manual.) My son could end up in college eating peanut butter sandwiches. Can you imagine his first job interview -- over lunch? Oh, the shame of it all!

Somehow, someway, Stephen needed to broaden his eating habits and I was determined to help him change.

A showdown was brewing! We pulled into a restaurant. I ordered the food and brought a hamburger and set it before my son. "Stephen, I didn't bring a peanut butter sandwich. Why don't you eat this hamburger?"

That determined look appeared on his face. "No! I want my peanut butter sandwich!"

"Son, there will be no peanut butter sandwich today. You are going to eat this hamburger!" As father and son squared off in a quiet restaurant, I recalled an old sales lesson. In a battle of stares the one who looks away first? Loses! This time, I would not, could not and dared not lose! Slowly, with a tear trickling down his cheek, he picked up the hamburger and took his first bite. His face slowly changed from a frown to a slight smile. Then he took a second bite and a third. Wow! As Mikey would say: "He liked it! He really liked it!"

Is there a point to this story?

Of course, there is. My son settled for the security of peanut butter and overlooked a smorgasbord of delectable food to savor. In many ways, don't we all? We seek security and pass on new opportunities, which although involving risks, also lead to golden opportunities. He complains about his job but never goes back to school to acquire new skills. She says: "I'm lonely" and stays home watching TV.

Next: From Peanut Butter Sandwiches to Faith and Ministry

July 15 - Breaking the Peanut Butter Habit – Conclusion

John 4:1-42

My son settled for the security of peanut butter and overlooked a smorgasbord of delectable food to savor. In many ways, don't we all? We seek security and pass on new opportunities, which although involving risks, also lead to golden opportunities.

Many of our churches cry out, "We want to be alive! We want to grow in our faith! We want to receive new families! We want a youth ministry! We want to make a difference in the world!" Yet so few churches are willing to venture beyond what they know is safe.

It's time to break the Peanut Butter habit!

For many years, I served as a pastor of small, medium, and large churches. At times, just like my son, we stubbornly clung to our peanut butter habits, our old ways. But at other times we took risks and God blessed us. Sometimes our risks worked, sometimes they didn't. But in the end, we grew stronger as we sampled God's amazing menu.

Jesus said: "I have food you don't know about. My nourishment comes from doing the will of God. Look around! Vast fields are ripening and are ready for the harvest. The harvesters are paid good wages and the fruit they harvest is people brought to eternal life. What joy awaits both the planter and the harvester alike!" (John 4:31-36)

- Jesus has a great menu waiting for us -
- We receive nourishment doing the will of God -
- Vast Fields are ripening all around you -
- The fruit will be people brought to eternal life -
- What joy awaits the planter and harvester alike -

Look at all the promises of good food! Are you settling for a peanut butter sandwich when God offers so much more? Maybe it's time to take a hard look at your relationship with God and with your church?

- Venture out and sign up for a Bible study.
- Join a small group that meets to offer godly encouragement.
- Volunteer to help a neighbor in need.
- Help with a mission or ministry project.
- Set aside more time for prayer.

Why settle for peanut butter when God offers: steak, lobster, salads, chocolate cake and pizza. Well, you get the picture and I'm getting hungry!

Prayer Challenge: What peanut butter habits do you need to change?

July 16 - Courage and Foolishness

1 Samuel chapter 17

It takes a lot of courage, to put things in God's hands,
To give ourselves completely, our lives, our hopes, our plans.
To follow where God leads us and make His will our own.
But all it takes is foolishness, to go the way alone!   -- Anonymous

Courage and Foolishness: The difference between the two is minimal. What is courage to some is foolishness to others. Remember David and Goliath? David's the kid with a few stones and a sling shot who nailed Goliath, with a rock between the eyes. We say David has courage because we know the ending of the story: Goliath struts, David lets fly the stone, Goliath falls, David wins! Break out the champagne and celebrate! But how would you feel had you been there?

"It takes a lot of courage to put things in God's hands." A nine-foot-tall monster taunts you to come and fight. Day after day you watch this ugly brute march up to your camp and insult you and your God. His threats and taunts produce the desired result: fear. You want to do something. You want to stand up to this threat. You want to do what is right but instead, you watch and wait.

"To give ourselves completely, our lives, our hope, our plans." Who are the giants in your life? We all have them. It may be a person, or pressure on the job, or problems in the family, but to you it is a giant. And this giant does not come out once. It comes relentlessly day after day. How do you react? Do you run? Do you give-in? Do you compromise? You want to react with courage, but then you stop and think, "Who am I to deal with a problem this big? Why should I be different from everyone else?" This isn't courage. It's foolishness.

"To follow where God leads us and make His will our own." All odds were against David, but he was not intimidated by Goliath. David always seemed to keep in mind that no matter how big the giants may be, God is always greater. We can all say that, but when the chips were down, David believed it and trusted in God to see him through. Can you? Is your faith in God big enough?

"But all it takes is foolishness, to go the way alone!" There is no guarantee that David will always defeat Goliath. Rather it is David's willingness to do what is right, wherever that leads. God honors that kind of courage. God will honor you when you truly see that even a giant like Goliath is a dwarf standing next to God.

It takes a lot of courage to put things in God's hands. To give ourselves completely, our lives, our hope, our plans. To follow where God leads us and make His will our own. But all it takes is foolishness, to go the way alone!

Prayer Challenge: What giants are you facing today? Give them to God.

July 17 - David and Revenge

1 Samuel chapter 24, Romans 12:14-21

Tolstoy wrote about a peasant who spent the night in a local inn. Someone was brutally murdered, and the murderer placed the weapon in the bag of the sleeping peasant. The police discovered it and put the hapless peasant in jail. For twenty-six years the peasant survived the harsh conditions of prison on the bitter hope that someday he would obtain revenge.

Then, the real murderer was placed in prison and was caught attempting to escape. One prisoner witnessed everything: the peasant. At long last the opportunity he had dreamed about since that dreadful night twenty-six years ago presented itself. For on the peasant's word the murderer would be put to death. Here was his chance to obtain the revenge he had long sought.

Revenge! "Don't get mad, get even!" Maybe an employer treated you unfairly or a coworker climbed to the top over your back. A spouse abandoned you. Your parents failed you. You were "done wrong" as they say and now you are looking to retaliate. "Don't get mad, get even." The Bible calls revenge, vengeance and has something to say: "Dear friends, never avenge yourselves. Leave that to God. For it is written, "I will take vengeance;" (Romans 12:19)

Personally, I would alter the language and say: "Occasionally avenge." Certainly, there should be exceptions for extreme examples such as our Russian peasant. I would say occasionally but I would be wrong. God says clearly, "never avenge."

A good Biblical example would be David.
King Saul was insanely jealous of David's increasing popularity and eventually stripped him of his job, his wife, his best friend, and his self-respect, finally forcing him to flee for safety. For years not days, Saul pursued David looking to exterminate him. One day while pursuing David, "Saul went into a cave to relieve himself. But as it happened, David and his men were hiding in that very cave!" (1 Samuel 24:3)

What would you do? "'Now's your opportunity!' David's men whispered to him."

So... David crept forward and cut off a piece of Saul's robe.

What? Why did David do that? Saul was trying to kill him. Why not get even? Instead, he crept close to Saul and performed the equivalent of a teenage prank or practical joke? Even that small act of defiance made David feel guilty. "The LORD knows I shouldn't have done it," he said." Yet, David's refusal to succumb to the temptation of getting even was a turning point in his life? Why?

Next: Answers and alternatives for seeking vengeance.

July 18 - David and Revenge - Conclusion

1 Samuel chapter 24, Romans 12:14-21

David had the opportunity to get even with King Saul after years of abuse. Yet, David chose another way. In the military, it is drilled into you: 'salute the rank, not the person.' Saul was anointed by God as King. David was duty bound to treat the King with honor. David would wisely choose mercy, not vengeance.

As Saul left the cave, David appeared and held up a piece of his robe. "This proves that I am not trying to harm you and that I have not sinned against you, even though you have been looking to kill me. The LORD will decide between us. Perhaps the LORD will punish you for what you are trying to do to me, but I will never harm you."

David's refusal to succumb to the temptation of "getting even" was a turning point in his life, because he chose to repay evil with good. "If your enemies are hungry, feed them. If they are thirsty, give them something to drink. Don't let evil get the best of you but conquer evil by doing good." (Romans 12:20-21)

David ultimately chose to place his faith in God and not to seek revenge. If you are treated unfairly, can you still project a loving and forgiving response toward the one who harmed you? That is the best witness of your integrity and faith.

Remember the Russian peasant in the story I mentioned earlier? He had his own opportunity to "get even" with the man who ruined his life. But instead of jumping at the chance, the story describes the peasant as experiencing the overpowering grace and love of God. The darkness within was filled with light and the peasant found himself saying to the officers: "I saw nothing."

That night the murderer approached the peasant and begged for forgiveness. Again, the light of Christ flooded the peasant's heart: "God will forgive you. Maybe I am a hundred times worse." And at saying those words, the peasant's heavy heart grew light as he received God's comfort.

I don't know of any better witness to your faith in God than a willingness to forgive someone who has grievously harmed you.

Is it easy? Never! Is it necessary and worthwhile? Absolutely! Your willingness to forgive could be the principal turning point in your life, your health, your faith and ultimately could be the best witness of your character and faith. Never avenge yourself. Leave that to God!

Prayer Challenge: God help me practice and model forgiveness.

July 19 - Curse of the Pink Flamingos

Psalm 95

I am being held captive by insidious members of our church youth group. As the esteemed writer Dave Berry would say: "I am not making this up!" Also, my humble apologies to the Flamingo Lawn Ornament Preservation Society, commonly referred to as F.L.O.P.S. I realize there are wonderful, wholesome benefits to having flamingo lawn ornaments in your yard and any future remarks should be considered tacky, ugly, and serve no benefit as they were made under duress.

It all started when I was asked to read to our church the following announcement by the same ruthless youth group now holding me hostage: "Beware! There is an affliction in our church! At any time, at any hour, at any moment, your yard is in jeopardy of being saturated with tacky, ugly, pink flamingos. Think about your usual morning routine; comfortable and relaxed. You calmly go to pick up the morning paper and there in your front yard are those bright, plastic, pink flamingos! Oh, the shame!"

The announcement continued: "But don't despair! There is hope in the air! We are the Flamingo Busters! Quick as a flash, before you can say, 'Get these pink flamingos out of my yard!'" our Flamingo Busters are ready to respond. For a sizable fee we will remove the tacky and distasteful affliction from your property. Or, better yet, buy our new **'No Pink Flamingos in My Yard'** insurance policy and we will protect your property from these pink destroyers. In other words: pay a little now or pay more later!"

I read the announcement. But then I paused and added, "These pink flamingo threats don't intimidate me. I refuse to buy insurance or give-in to these cheap theatrical tricks." While speaking, I noticed two people running over to the youth to buy insurance.

The next morning an email announced: "The Pink Flamingo reign of terror has begun!" "Oh no," I screamed and ran outside. There were fifteen pink flamingos in all their glory perched in my front yard. I dialed Flamingo Busters and did the only noble thing a poor preacher could do. I begged them to come immediately and remove those pink, ugly birds from my yard! They came but before removing the pink terror, they tied me up and forced me to write this story so everyone will know of the Pink Flamingo Affliction.

Psalm 95 begins: Come, let us sing to the Lord! Let us give a joyous shout to the rock of our salvation! Let us come before him with thanksgiving. Let us sing psalms of praise. For the Lord is a great God... (1-3)

A Daily Dose of Godly Encouragement: Medicine for Tough Days

Be honest, when was the last time you heard a joyous shout in your home, in your office, at your school or in your church? Expressing joy with creativity and imagination is part of our service to God. No group expresses joy in more creative ways than our youth. (Remember, I'm still tied up.) Recently, they led one of our worship services. There was creative dancing, flags, thought-provoking drama, and lots of participation.

I learned two things: One: Look for joy in serving God. If your home or church seems lacking, then look for innovative ways to add your own style of joy. Two: Don't overlook the contribution of our youth. They can restore joy in us all. One more thing: If someone offers to sell you "No Pink Flamingos in My Yard" Insurance? Buy it!

Prayer Challenge: Pray for creative outbursts of joy in your home and church.

July 20 - Journey Church

Psalm 107:23-32

Psalm 107:23-32 uses the example of ships going out to sea as a lesson on risk taking. "Those who dare to risk greatly by going out on the mighty waters will see the works of the Lord, his wonderful deeds in the deep." In earlier times, going out to sea was highly risky. Many ships left port never to return. Storms, mishaps, disease, and attacks by pirates were frequent and deadly. Yet for those willing to risk there was a promise of enormous riches. People returned with stories of spectacular sights and miracles witnessed. Today, a willingness to take risks, can affect how we play sports, how we manage our career, how we talk to others and how we live out our faith in God.

I visited a risk-taking church that began as a thrift store. They were helping people financially, but they were also providing spiritual aid. The people who were helped had difficulties finding a church to live out their newfound faith. So, the leaders who started the thrift store sailed for deeper waters and created Journey United Methodist Church.

One Sunday, I decided to visit this risk-taking church. The first thing I noticed as I drove up was a guy in the parking lot waving at passing cars on the nearby highway. When I asked why, he said: "My call from God is to wave at and pray for every car that passes our church. It doesn't matter whether they come inside or not. God wants me to wave and pray." As I entered there were two signs: "Sorry, the store is closed but the Church is Open!" followed by: "Journey Church Enter Here."

After passing through rooms filled with clothes, household goods and furniture I entered a large room that was formerly a garage. Everyone was busy, friendly, and excited. Just before the service began, we gathered to pray for each other, for the people about to come and for the community. "Lord, use us to do your will." As people came, they were greeted warmly with handshakes and hugs. They were offered juice and coffee, donuts and bagels and encouraged to mingle and enjoy. The worship leader warmly greeted everyone and explained how Journey began and what would happen during worship. In addition to the music, the prayers and the message, there would also be time for discussion based on how we could live out the message in our daily lives.

One person at the service told me that when he was in the hospital, several of the members of this church surrounded his bed and prayed for him. He wasn't interested in attending church at the time but he's here now. Another spoke of going through a difficult marriage and divorce. She drifted away from her church and from God. Several members of this church visited her and encouraged her. In a culture where more churches close than open, Journey is a huge risk. A ship sailing into deep and mighty waters. But Journey has become a powerful witness for God. The risk of failure remains but whether they succeed or fail, Journey has changed many lives.

William Ward writes: "To laugh is to risk being a fool. To weep is to risk appearing sentimental. To reach out to another is to risk involvement. To expose feelings is to risk rejections. To place your dreams before others is to risk ridicule. To love is to risk not being loved in return. To go forward in the face of overwhelming odds is to risk failure."

"But risks must be taken because the greatest hazard in life is to risk nothing. The person who risks nothing does nothing and accomplishes nothing. One may avoid risking, that could result in suffering and sorrow but to do so prohibits learning, change, growth, and love. A person who takes risks is set free to live."

Prayer Challenge: Read Psalm 107 and pray for courage to sail into deeper waters.

July 21 - FreeCell

Philippians 3:12-16

On any computer with Windows, you will find the card game, 'FreeCell.' When I come to a stopping place at work, I play a quick game.' When faced with a tough situation, I'll pause for another round. When I'm feeling good or when I have a few minutes, I'll whip out "FreeCell." According to Microsoft, "The object of FreeCell is to move the cards to the home area, using free cells as placeholders." The rules then add a mysterious extra note: "It is believed (although not proven) that every game is winnable." Really?

Maybe every game is winnable for a genius but not for me. Sometimes a game is so easy, anyone can play: the cards seem to fall into place. Sometimes you can look ahead and make a calculated move or two. Sometimes you make a mistake or a dumb move and end up defeating yourself. Sometimes despite your best efforts the game proves too challenging, forcing you to quit.

More often, you are in a tight spot and one or two moves away from disaster. You've reached a turning point. The temptation is to give up. It would be easier to start over but if you quit, you lose. However, if you refuse to give up: stop for a moment, regroup your thoughts and approach the game with a fresh dose of creativity you will often be rewarded with renewed insight resulting in a small correction that leads to a series of good moves resulting in an immensely satisfying victory.

But "FreeCell" also offers life lessons. Sometimes, everything in life seems so easy, and our decisions turn out right. Sometimes, we only need to make a few good choices to keep things going smoothly. Sometimes, we make a mistake or do something dumb that causes an obvious setback. And sometimes, despite our best efforts everything seems too challenging, forcing us to start over.

Sometimes, we are in a tight spot and one or two moves away from disaster. We've reached a turning point. The temptation is to give up. It would be easier to start over but if you quit, you lose. But if you refuse to give up: stop for a moment, regroup your thoughts, then approach your situation with a fresh dose of creativity you will often be rewarded with renewed insight resulting in a small correction that leads to a series of good moves resulting in an immensely satisfying victory.

The promise of Scripture is: "I strain to reach the end of the race and receive the prize for which God, through Christ Jesus, is calling us up to heaven." Consistent winners within the journey of life and faith refuse to quit when facing turning points. They turn to God, continue to explore other options, and turn potential disaster into ministry opportunities and even miracles. Whether it's 'FreeCell' or life: Keep working toward that day. Forget the past and look forward. Strain to reach the end of the race because God through Jesus Christ is calling us up to heaven. "FreeCell" anyone?

Prayer Challenge: Whatever you may be facing, refuse to quit! Look to God!

July 22 - Ten Questions

Romans chapter 12

People often ask: "Larry, am I doing what God wants me to do?" I use ten questions to regularly guide me as a pastor and to guide the spiritual life of the church I serve. So maybe you will find the questions helpful too. Warning: Don't think you have to check everything or feel guilty about what you are not doing. These questions are simply meant to be a practical guide for you and your church.

Do you pray regularly? It sounds so simple, yet nothing happens without prayer. Personal struggles often seem magnified when your prayer life slacks off. Does your church emphasize prayer as a regular and critical part of ministry? Prayer should always be step one.

Do you have a vision? It is difficult to shoot an arrow when there is no target. So how can you function without a vision followed by goals to help you fulfill the vision? What talents and resources are available to you and your church? What ministry is needed in your community?

Are we growing in faith? Spiritual formation is a continuous journey of learning, experiencing, and sharing the Word of God. Young and old are discovering a passion for God's Word but don't always know where to begin. Bible studies and small groups play a key role in spiritual development. You can start a Bible study, participate in a small group, or join a prayer ministry.

Are you caring for others? What are you doing to maintain loving contact with friends and family? Do you regularly offer encouragement to friends, coworkers, or neighbors? What is your church doing to care for each other? Most churches offer life groups, support ministries or prayer chains. Perhaps you can join in. Even the simple gesture of sending a card is a ministry which often works miracles.

Do you cultivate friendships above and below your age? It's important to reach beyond your comfort level and seek to understand other age groups and cultures. You learn a lot and you can have a great time doing it. Young and old alike have so much to offer but need our love, encouragement, and respect.

These first questions can strengthen your connection with God and deepen your interaction with people around you. As you work to answer them, you may find God guiding you with encouragement and ideas. Write them down and refer to them later.

Next: Five more questions moving from faith to ministry.

July 23 - Ten Questions - Conclusion

First Corinthians chapters 12 & 13

Are you involved in a community ministry? Habitat for Humanity, the food bank or a local hospital all offer wonderful ministry opportunities. How about children at Christmas? Are groups fixing broken down houses for people too poor or sickly to make their own repairs? There is "Meals on Wheels." Every community has needs. To meet them God gave us unique talents. What are you doing with yours? Discover what's needed and ask: "How can I help?" What a difference you could make!

Are you a witness? Do people know what you believe? How do you talk about God without others feeling intimidated or offended? Do coworkers look at you as someone they can trust? Do you listen to their concerns with respect and love? Are you praying for opportunities to share your faith? My favorite definition of witness is the willingness to make a sincere and honest attempt to be a friend to someone in the name of God.

What about men? More than 60% of those not attending church are men. Mission trips, building projects and sports have all proven to be successful ways to include guys. Many come back to participate in other activities. One church provided a steak dinner for men. I like that! But men also need a friend, someone who cares and will listen.

Are we reaching single adults? A large percentage of our population is single. Surveys indicate many single adults believe in God but feel isolated from church. We recognize their needs by changing our language. Family night supper implies you should be married. Try "Fellowship and Fun" suppers. Ministry ideas include divorce and grief recovery workshops. Provide free childcare for stressed out single parents.

What about children? Parents struggle to provide a wholesome environment. You can start by enthusiastically volunteering at Sunday school as a teacher or volunteer. There are other opportunities such as: After-School Ministry or MOPS (Mothers of Pre-Schoolers.) Any church offering ministry for children also needs willing and able volunteers. You can be a witness and a source of encouragement for a child.

"I can't possibly do all that!" True but you can do something. My prayer is for these questions to stimulate your thinking. Then, let God guide you. We all face a challenge to reach out in creative ways. Be open-minded, be in prayer and celebrate victories.

The biggest joy of my life has been to witness people inspired by God become more involved in ministry.

The excitement of doing something worthwhile for God is more contagious than a flu epidemic and the results are far more lasting and satisfying. So, what are you waiting for? Start praying about how to respond to these ten questions and may God guide you and inspire you!

Prayer Challenge: Include these ten questions in your prayer time.

July 24 – Modern Day Disciples

Matthew 22:34-40, 28:16-20

Trish is a divorced single parent. She has a demanding, stress-filled job and is trying to raise two children. She once attended church but no longer has time. She was hoping to receive encouragement from her church but after the separation, no one called.

Richard experienced several job changes. The job he has now doesn't pay nearly what he used to receive. He used to attend church regularly but when his job problems began, he could no longer give what he pledged. Embarrassed, he stopped attending.

Phil and Judy have two young children. They are considering attending a local church but haven't followed through. Meanwhile, their next-door neighbors drive off every Sunday morning dressed up to go to church but so far have not invited Phil and Judy.

How can we be the church for Trish, Richard, Phil, and Judy? One religious consultant confessed: "I was taught to make and train members of a church. Instead, I should have been teaching disciples for Christ." What does that mean? In the Bible, a disciple asks: "Teacher, which is the most important commandment in the law of Moses?"

Jesus replied, "You must love the Lord your God with all your heart, all your soul, and all your mind. This is the first and greatest commandment. A second is equally important: 'Love your neighbor as yourself. The entire law and all the demands of the prophets are based on these two commandments." (Mat. 22:36-40) Disciples of Jesus learn to ask: How can we love the Lord our God with all our heart, all our soul and all our mind and what would it mean for us to love our neighbor as much as we love ourselves?

Remember Trish, our divorced, single parent? She was invited by a coworker to a divorce recovery meeting at a nearby church: meals and childcare provided. Trish never felt more secure and loved. Weeks later, she and her children attended worship at the same church. Now, Trish is a leader in the divorce recovery ministry of that church.

Richard, who experienced financial difficulties renewed his friendship with a buddy on Facebook. With his friend's encouragement, Richard visited a men's breakfast group at his church. Richard was pleasantly surprised to be warmly welcomed and discovered that many of the men experienced similar struggles. Now, Richard is one of the cooks at the men's group and leads a group that offers classes to help those who lost their jobs.

Judy received a tweet mentioning a MOPS group. MOPS stands for Mothers of Pre-Schoolers, a faith-based group offering support for mothers and their children. Days later, she attended one of their gatherings and found practical advice and an atmosphere of encouragement. While there she was invited to attend worship. Now, Phil and Judy volunteer with the children's ministry at that same church.

Yes, the world has changed dramatically but the church can still make a difference in the midst of those changes. Just ask Trish, Richard, Judy, and Phil.

Prayer Challenge: Lord, help me learn to become more of a disciple.

July 25 - Flashlights & The Beatitudes

Matthew 5:1-16

Jesus says, *"You are the light of the world."* (Matthew 5:14) What does that mean? Jesus says this in his sermon immediately following what we call the Beatitudes. Maybe the verses are connected?

I found a flashlight in a junk drawer. I can use the flashlight to illustrate how applying the Beatitudes helps us to be a light to the world. I'll flick this switch and... Hey! What's wrong with my flashlight? It worked great before. Lesson: It's hard to be a light to the world while sitting around unused.

"Blessed are those who realize they are helpless and put their trust in God."

The batteries must be dead. I'll just open the flashlight and... oh no! The flashlight is full of shoestrings, paper clips, matches and toothpicks. How in the world did all this trash get in my flashlight? Lesson: It's hard to be a light when your guts are full of trash.

"Blessed are those who passionately care about others. Blessed are those who in humility allow God to control their passion and anger."

Okay the trash is out so now I put the flashlight back together and make my point. What were those words again? "Let there be light!" Now what? I cleaned out the trash. Why won't my light shine? Oops! I forgot the batteries. Lesson: It's hard to be a light when you have no power.

"Blessed are those who long to follow God with their own heart."

The trash is out, and the batteries are in. Here we go. "Let there be light!" Hooray! It works! My light is shining! Now... where do I shine the light? Lesson: It's hard to be a light when you don't know where to shine. "Blessed are those who truly understand others feelings and concerns.

"Blessed are those who keep their motives and actions pure. Blessed are those who can help to heal the conflicts between people and nations. Blessed are those who are willing to suffer for what they believe."

The flashlight and the beatitudes help me see more clearly what needs to be done. My Bible is looking dusty. Next door is a retired couple I've never met. Across the street is a single mom with automobile problems. My church needs volunteers to help with their youth. I can't do it all, but I can do something. Lord, keep my flashlight shining and help me to be your light to the world.

Prayer Challenge: Help my light shine brightly so others see You more clearly.

July 26 - Healing Service

John chapter 9

After a short introduction to Dot, an energetic 75-year-old. She said: "I'm taking you to a 'real' church!" Dot felt led by God to provide lodging for me during my studies at seminary. But before I could put down my suitcase, she led me outside to her car.

"As Jesus was walking along, he saw a man blind from birth." (John 9:1)

As we entered the crowded church everyone was singing and clapping exuberantly. We were ushered to seats directly in front of the speakers. It had been just a few short weeks since leaving the business world to become a preacher. Yet here I was on the front row of a crowded worship service having no idea what was going on. Dot smiled and gave me a look that implied, "Trust me."

"'Teacher,' his disciples asked him, 'why was this man born blind?' Jesus answered. 'He was born blind so the power of God could be seen in him." (2-3)

The music was energetic and easy to sing. The speaker stressed the importance of individual fasting and prayer. "We cannot be an example for others unless we are willing to practice what we believe!" he said.

"Then Jesus spat on the ground, made mud with the saliva, and smoothed the mud over the blind man's eyes. He told him, 'Go and wash in the pool of Siloam. So, the man went and washed and came back seeing!" (6-7)

The preacher pointed to a woman and talked of a recent divorce and how God would help her cope as a single mother. He spoke to a young man about struggles with alcoholism. Then, the minister looked directly at me and asked me to stand. He told everyone I was a new minister and asked everyone to pray for my ministry.

"His neighbors and others who knew him as a blind beggar asked each other, 'Is this the same man - that beggar? Some said he was and others said, 'No, but he surely looks like him.' And the beggar kept saying, 'I am the same man!'" (8-9)

People began moving toward the front. The minister approached a woman and mentioned a severe blood disorder. "In the name of Jesus, heal her!" he said. The woman spread her arms into the air, screamed and fell back... right into my arms. Two women came and gently eased her to the floor.

I left the service with more questions than answers: Are healing services necessary for God to respond? What about people who are not healed? What does it mean for a church to be involved in a healing ministry?

Next: Answers.

July 27 - Healing Service - Conclusion

John chapter 9

A healing service left me confused and filled with questions: Are special services necessary for God to heal? Was the woman at the service healed of a blood disorder simply because hands were placed on her? What about those who are not healed?

I asked several leaders of our church to join me in looking into the miracle of God's healing. We gathered as a group looking to find answers. Our first step was to study scripture. We discovered four basic but critical lessons.

1. God heals: "He forgives my sins and heals my diseases - " (Psalm 103.3)
2. Jesus healed: "- and Jesus healed all the sick." (Matthew 8:17)
3. The disciples healed: "Jesus sent them out to heal the sick." (Luke 9:2)
4. We heal: "Are any among you sick? They should call for the elders and have them pray and their prayer offered in faith will heal the sick." (James 5:14-15)

We invited other churches to talk about their healing ministry. We learned that we are already involved with healing. Every time we visit someone, send a card, deliver a basket of food, offer a prayer, we are offering God's miracle of healing. Our task was to learn how to improve our existing healing ministry.

We learned that healing is a miracle and an example of God's mercy, not a performance. Healing involves spiritual and emotional wholeness as much as a physical act. Healing occurs in God's way, in God's time. Healing includes responses such as nursing care, counseling, and acts of kindness. Healing may mean courage to endure suffering and hardship rather than instant reprieve. Healing ultimately means our earthly death is a victory ensuring eternal life in heaven.

"Jesus went to the blind man and asked, 'Do you believe in the Son of Man?' The man answered, 'Who is he, sir, because I would like to.' Jesus said, 'You have seen him, and he is speaking to you!' The blind man responded, 'Yes, Lord, I believe!' And he worshiped Jesus." (John 9:35-39)

After preparation and prayer our church leaders shared what we discovered and how we hoped to expand our healing ministry from increasing our visitation ministry to providing training for one of our members to become a Parish Nurse.

At the end of the final service, after months of preparation, several leaders stood with me as I offered the opportunity for anyone who needed prayer for healing to come forward. In the background a musician began playing softly. For the longest moment, nothing happened -- Then the miracle of God's healing began.

First one woman needed help in dealing with Osteoporosis. Right behind her was another person suffering from chronic back problems. A man confessed his addiction to prescription medication. The line grew as we gathered around each person, heard their request, and offered prayers. At one point the music stopped and for several minutes, all you could hear were the sounds of people sobbing while others prayed for them.

In my many years of ministry, I seldom witnessed such a spiritual and emotional outpouring. Over the next few days, several who came forward told me of dramatic changes and yes -- even miracles! Understanding and believing the miracle of God's healing was a critical turning point in the ministry of our church.

Have I successfully answered all the questions and concerns about healing? No and I likely never will, but like the healed blind man, I can now emphatically say to Jesus and to you: "Yes Lord, I believe! I was blind and now I see!"

Prayer Challenge: Help me understand and appreciate the miracle of healing.

July 28 - A Healing Story

Luke 9:1-6

Anne was in the hospital with an unknown infection in her knees and hips that was so severe, she had not been able to get out of bed for nearly a year. At the young age of forty-two, she was not only facing severe infection and extensive surgery but also a mountain of personal problems including drug abuse, family squabbles and a stack of unpaid bills. Anne was in a lot of trouble.

Routine blood tests in preparation for surgery revealed an added horror for our forty-two-year-old sufferer. Anne was HIV positive and would likely develop full-blown symptoms of AIDS. I accompanied the doctor as she explained HIV/AIDS and the ramifications. Then the doctor left. For nearly an hour Anne alternately talked and cried. She had been horribly abused much of her life. The years of beatings, brutal sexual abuse and drugs took their toll. At one point, Anne was filled with rage: at her family who abused her, her so-called friends who used her and even God for seemingly abandoning her. Soon she would face excruciating surgery followed by a long, painful recovery only to then face the reality of HIV/AIDS.

What could I say? I listened, tried to understand, and cried with her. At some point, I felt led to ask: "Anne, would you like to receive Holy Communion?"

She looked at me for the longest time. Then with the slightest trace of a smile amid all those tears, Anne nodded and said: "Yes, please." Later, that night, amidst the busyness and noise of a large metropolitan hospital a student chaplain and a deeply troubled woman, together discovered the words of comfort only God can give: "Merciful God, we confess that we have not loved you with our whole heart. Forgive us we pray. Free us for joyful obedience, through Jesus Christ our Lord. In the name of Jesus Christ, you are forgiven. Christ has died; Christ is risen; Christ will come again. The body of Christ, given for you. The blood of Christ given for you. Amen."

I don't know why God physically heals some people and not others. Why do some endure more pain than any one person can possibly bear? Maybe we're asking the wrong question. The right question might be: Where is God during our troubles? Can we anticipate a future beyond the suffering we experience now?

Several days later, following her knee and hip surgery, I was summoned to Anne's room. She grasped my hand, looked at me and said: "I sensed the presence of God in the room that night during communion and for the first time in my life I felt truly loved. Thank you! I have a surprise for you!" She got out of the hospital bed and stood up. Anne then asked me to escort her on the first walk she had taken in over a year. Together we walked the length of the hospital corridor and back. This time it was my turn to cry.

Prayer Challenge: Lord, help me better appreciate your awesome gift of grace.

July 29 - Storms & Lighthouses

Psalm 27

One Sunday morning I called all the children to the front and told them a story: "It is a dark and stormy night." (The room becomes dark.) "Lightning flashes across the sky." (Various lights begin blinking.) "The wind is howling." (Sounds of a storm fill the room.) "The ship is tossed about." (Everyone starts swaying from side to side.)

Here is the best part: "Huge waves crash overhead." (I squirt the children with a spray bottle.) Can you picture what's happening? Children are squealing and laughing. There's total chaos in the room as the storm continues to rage and the children shout with me: "We're drowning! Help! Who will save us?"

Then I say: "God gives us a miracle. Look! Up ahead! What's that?" (In the far corner of the room a light begins to shine.) "It's a light -- from a lighthouse! We're saved! We were lost and now we are found!"

What a great lesson. After all, could anything offer more hope and direction to a ship caught in the grip of a fierce storm than the bright, steady beam of light from a lighthouse? What could provide more comfort than that reassuring glow: a light to guide you safely home? "Lord, you have brought light to my life; my

God, you light up my darkness." (Psalm 18:28) Like a lighthouse, God offers the light of direction to lead me out of darkness.

"The Lord is my light and my salvation – so why should I be afraid?" (Psalm 27:1) Like a lighthouse, God offers the light of salvation to rescue us from the storms of life. "I am the light of the world. If you follow me, you won't be stumbling through the darkness, because you will have the light that leads to life." (John 8:12) Like a lighthouse, God offers all of us a strong steady light that leads to life.

Have you experienced a few dark and stormy nights complete with lightning flashes and howling winds? Do you occasionally feel like a helpless ship tossed about with huge waves crashing overhead? Maybe now is the time to turn toward the eternal light: "Look! Up ahead! What's that?" (In the quiet corner of your soul a light begins to shine.) "It's a light, from The Lighthouse! We are saved! We were lost and now we are found!"

If you are going through storms, if you are searching for purpose, if you are seeking a new ministry, if you want to deepen your relationship with God. What could possibly provide more comfort than the reassuring glow of a lighthouse promising to be, "A light to guide you safely home?"

Prayer Challenge: How has God been a Lighthouse for you?

July 30 - Bad Day!

1 Peter 1:3-9

I received the following email: "It has been a BEAR of a day! I received a ticket for an expired inspection sticker, in the midst of other problems: losing my job, divorce and being forced to move. Yesterday, I received notice that my license was suspended! So, I promptly went down to the courthouse to pay the fine. A police officer pulled me over because I was driving with an expired license plate."

Have you ever had days, months or even years that start badly and then get worse? Where problems add up, then multiply? You reach the floor of difficulties only to discover a basement of woe? So, how does God help us?

Peter offered reassurance when feeling overwhelmed. "Be truly glad! There is joy ahead, even though it is necessary for you to endure trials for a while. These trials are only to test your faith, to show that it is strong and pure. It is being tested as fire purifies gold – and your faith is far more precious to God than mere gold. So, if your faith remains strong after being tried by fiery trials, it will bring you much praise and glory and honor on the day when Jesus Christ is revealed to the whole world. (1 Peter 1:6-7)

Be truly glad while enduring a really bad day? Sounds crazy, but I found crucial lessons offering enduring hope:

- Really bad days must be endured but there is a promise of joy ahead.
- Really bad days strengthen your faith just as fire purifies gold.
- Really bad days produce a tested faith more precious than gold.
- Really bad days will bring you praise, glory and honor in heaven.

What ultimately matters to God is our continued and tested faith strengthened and purified by our pain and struggle. How we learn to cope with bad days often shapes our outlook on life and defines our relationship with God. How we overcome bad days represents our witness to the outside world.

Is it easy? Of course not! This is why we need to continually pursue a deeper relationship with God. The promise of God is the bad days will be forgotten as we bask in the praise, glory and honor of heaven.

Prayer Challenge: Lord, give me strength and perspective during my bad days.

July 31 - Six Strong Men

Romans chapter 12

A newspaper ad showed a black and white photograph of six men carrying a coffin through the front doors of a church. The caption: "Will it take six strong men to bring you back to church?" My first reaction was shock, but the ad made me pause and think. What about you? Why won't more people attend church regularly?

Here is what I often hear: *I'm too busy. The sermons are dull and the music is old-fashioned. Church people are such hypocrites. I'd rather watch TV and stay home. They only want money. I'm young, divorced or poor. They don't want me.*

For years, my excuse for not attending church: *"I work six days a week in a suit and tie. I want to sleep-in, relax and read the paper."* Truthfully, I just did not feel any great need to be in church. Obviously, my situation changed but why?

Will it take six strong men to bring you back into the church?

Zig Ziglar, a well-known motivational speaker and author, literally sold me on the benefits of becoming a

Christian and attending church now instead of putting it off until later. Zig described the local church as the body of Christ showing me a piece of Heaven today, not just when we die. What is that piece of heaven? What are those benefits of attending church? I thought you would never ask:

Longer life: Insurance studies show regular church attendance adds years to your life. Wealth: The Bible is full of methods for effectively managing your money. Peace: There is peace of mind knowing God is there. Purpose: God has a purpose for you. Courage: God will give you courage to make ethical and moral decisions. Love: Loving others as God loves you is a source of happiness and comfort. Forgiveness: Learning to forgive yourself and others can literally heal your body and soul.

Why do we need to go to church? Because the church is still the best way to strengthen your relationship with God and with others, find your life's purpose and receive those special benefits.

My attitude changed. I found church to be the place where I would be strengthened during the other six days of the week. Yes, at times, I am busy, the music is awful, the preacher is boring, and people are hypocrites. But I discovered an indescribable love and peace. I found a source of encouragement and a place of acceptance.

Let's face it. You need the church, and the church needs you. If you've not been to church in a while? Come back. If you are active, share this story with a friend and invite him/her to join you. It sure beats the alternative offered by this ad. Ecch!!

Prayer Challenge: "Will it take six strong men to bring you back into the church?"

August

August 1 - Preacher Stories

1 Timothy chapter 6

A young man from our church was standing just outside the hospital smoking a cigarette but when he saw me, he seemed to panic. Suddenly he stuck the lit cigarette in his pants pocket and turned toward me with an innocent smile and said, "Hi preacher. How are you doing?"

I don't remember ever preaching on the evils of smoking so why did he do that? I was curious to see what would happen next. Would smoke come out of his pants? Would he grimace in pain trying to squeeze the burning tobacco with his fingers? But nothing happened. After a few minutes, I said good-bye and moved on.

People say and do strange things around preachers. At wedding receptions where alcohol is served, people often hide their drinks when I walk by. One young lady literally tossed her drink, glass and all into the trash can as I walked in the room. Why? Are they afraid I might turn them in?

A young adult Sunday school class once discussed whether it was okay to drink alcohol. Everyone agreed that it was acceptable in moderation. A few admitted that drinking might be a poor witness to someone who struggled with addiction. But then I asked, "Would you be concerned if you saw me taking a drink?"

"Oh yes," they all said in horror! "Pastors can't drink!"

When I announced my intention to go into the ministry at a sales meeting, one associate looked horrified. After the meeting, he approached me and said: "Why didn't you tell me you were a preacher? I would never curse like that in front of you!"

Paul gave wise advice to a preacher: "Teach these truths and encourage everyone to obey them." (1 Timothy 6:2) This is the basic responsibility of a preacher: teach the truth and encourage others to obey. So, even though we are human and make lots of mistakes, we preachers are called by God to teach the truth, to lead by example and to encourage others in their walk of faith. Paul then writes: "Pursue a godly life, along with faith, love perseverance, and gentleness."

Pursuing a godly life is not just for preachers. Our best witness is in how we behave. As a minister, I try to set a good example. Next time you see me; don't stick a lit cigarette in your pocket or throw your drink in the trash can. Remember Jesus never commanded us to be perfect; He did say, "Follow Me!"

Prayer Challenge: How can we encourage each other in our walk with God?

August 2 - Halftimers

Luke 10:1-9

Uncle James was head of Parks and Recreation for a large city: a demanding job managing thousands of employees. Feeling the need to do more for God, he asked the leaders of his local church how he could become more involved. So, they asked him to serve on a committee. As he talked, I noticed the church never seemed interested in the job he managed every day: A job which impacted thousands. My Uncle was seeking a ministry, but the church put him on a committee.

James is not unusual. One recent trend in America is called "Halftime" named after the book by Bob Buford, describing people who desire something more in their life to enable them to move from financial and career success to achieve goals that are more significant or even spiritual. The issue is not whether people want something more significant in their life. We already know they do. The real question is how will the church respond? Will we help them find and develop a meaningful ministry or will we take the easy way out and put them on a committee?

What about you? God called you for a ministry. Do you know what it is? How should the church help?

Committee work is important but there is so much more. As a minister, I emphasize: A church should provide an atmosphere of encouragement for you to improve your relationship with God through worship, prayer, Bible study and small group participation. Then we should help you discover your unique talents and use them toward a ministry of helping others in your community and around the world.

"The Lord now chose seventy-two other disciples and sent them ahead in pairs to all the towns and villages he planned to visit. These were his instructions to them: 'The harvest is so great, and the workers are so few. Pray to the Lord who is in charge of the harvest and ask Him to send out more workers for his fields. Go now and remember that I am sending you out as lambs among wolves. Don't take along any money or a traveler's bag or even an extra pair of sandals.'" (Luke 10:1-4)

The Lord chose: You don't just decide to serve God. You were chosen. But what task were you chosen for? Are you doing it? **Travel in pairs:** God knows it's difficult to work alone. We need encouragement. **Pray for more workers:** Your life of prayer is just as important as your willingness to work. **Lambs among wolves:** Wolves see lambs as only one thing… supper. Serving God involves risk. **Travel lite:** Too much stuff, no matter how good, becomes a burden. Keep your message and your faith simple.

A minister wrote: "Life is like a dog race. You are forever chasing the rabbit. One day the rabbit stops in the middle of the race. Now what? There is bedlam as dogs yelp and bite each other." Are you running to achieve success but upon catching the rabbit, not knowing what to do next? Welcome to the potential of half-time.

Prayer Challenge: What ministry is God calling you? How can your church help?

August 3 - Half-Timers: Success to Significance

Romans chapter 12

Uncle James was seeking a ministry, but the church put him on a committee. James is a half-timer who desires to move from financial and career success to achieving goals more significant or spiritual. Here are a few half-timers I know: Al owns an insurance business and leads a ministry team at his church. Betsy retired as a school guidance counselor and now works for her church as a volunteer coordinator helping others become more involved. Polly retired from College Administration, joined mission work teams helping to rebuild houses. Vance sold his communication business and is now helping his church explore new ways of communicating the message of Christ.

Could you be a potential half-timer? Lloyd Reeb, of "From Success to Significance," provides questions: "I've been relatively successful. Is there more to life than my current situation? What do I consider eternally significant? What is my real purpose on earth? What would give my life more meaning? Did my first half experience lay a foundation for something more meaningful?"

Paul could be describing half-timers: "And so, dear brothers and sisters, I plead with you to give your bodies to God because of all he has done for you. Let them be a living and holy sacrifice—the kind he will find acceptable. This is truly the way to worship him. Don't copy the behavior and customs of this world, but let God transform you into a new person by changing the way you think. Then you will know God's will for you, which is good and pleasing and perfect." (Romans 12:1-2)

Half-timers see a need to give their bodies to Christ as a living and holy sacrifice. This is the way they choose to worship God. Instead of retiring or settling for the behavior and customs of the world, they allow God to transform them into a new person following God's will and moving from survival to success to significance.

If you are a potential half-timer, here are a few helpful steps provided by Lloyd Reeb: Write down what makes you most passionate. Pinpoint your three greatest natural abilities. Develop your personal mission statement. Define the position you best play on the team. Discover where your life needs better balance. Plan your finances with an eternal perspective. Set the five most important goals to live out your mission.

Maybe you are looking to make a change. I pray you will find someone who will take the time to listen and talk to you about the second half of your life. We should also be prayerfully alert for people and opportunities God sends our way.

Someone could approach you wanting to do more. Their idea or potential contribution could make a huge difference to you, to your church and to your community.

Prayer Challenge: How is God leading you to respond to this devotion?

August 4 - Rodney

First Corinthians chapter 12

A few years ago, I noticed the tv show, "Rodney" was taking place inside a church during worship. Curious, I waited to see what would happen next. The preacher was pacing the floor, shouting: "you must straighten up and get right with God now. Because if you don't -- do you know where you're going? Well, do you?"

"Hell!" The congregation shouted, with enthusiasm. He continued the dialogue shouting: Where? "Hell!" What did you say? "Hell!" Everyone was enthusiastically shouting except for poor Rodney who was quietly sinking deeper into the pew looking more and more -- lost. Later that day, panic-stricken Rodney drove to the preacher's house and knocked on the door. The Reverend trying to watch a ball game and obviously annoyed at the interruption reluctantly answered. "Please help me," pleads Rodney. "Don't let my family go to heaven without me. What should I do to be saved?"

Noticeably annoyed the preacher at first says, "Can you come back later?" Finding that doesn't work, he asks: "You'll do anything?" When Rodney nods his head, he continues: "You could cut my grass."

A Daily Dose of Godly Encouragement: Medicine for Tough Days

Ouch! Rodney is searching for an answer to one of life's deepest questions: "What can I do to have a restored relationship with God? How can I be forgiven my past and receive hope for the future?" And the preacher, the representative of God's church responds: "You could cut my grass?"

Rodney cut the grass for the preacher, then he cut the church grass. He would have cut anyone's grass if it helped but Rodney wanted to do more. The preacher then asked him to speak to a group of youth about sin. Rodney stood before the group and described his own sins: in graphic detail. The parents were horrified, the pastor was embarrassed, and poor Rodney was humiliated and more confused than ever. At this point, he didn't know what to do.

The preacher pulled him aside and rather than scold Rodney, he pleaded: "Can you forgive me? You came looking for help and instead of listening, I gave you chores and asked you to speak before a group when you were not ready. Why don't we go to lunch and talk about how to have a real relationship with God and what you can do next."

Maybe you are the one looking to make changes in your life. I pray that you will find someone who will take the time to listen and talk to you. As for the rest of us? We should prayerfully be alert for the people and opportunities God regularly sends our way. At any time, a Rodney could approach you or your church wanting to talk about God and making life-altering changes. Stop whatever you are doing and listen carefully. And please -- don't ask them to cut the grass.

Prayer Challenge: Whether you are like Rodney or the preacher, pray and be alert!

August 5 - Chairs

Proverbs 3:5-6

Worry is like a rocking chair. It will give you something to do but get you nowhere. Worry is like a disease. It infects everyone, yet no one seeks a cure. Most people wear their worry like a badge of honor. But surrendering to worry is dangerous enough to ruin your physical and spiritual vitality and drain your life of hope and joy. Yet, knowing all that, I still worry, a lot! Don't you? I worry over my wife, my children, and my grandchildren. I even worry about my faith. Isn't that silly?

Can we stop worrying? Probably not but we can learn to replace worry with trust. We learn about "trust" from Proverbs. Imagine a wise parent giving advice to a teenager and you begin to understand the message: "Trust in the Lord with all your heart; do not depend on your own understanding. Seek his will in all you do, and he will direct your paths." (3:5-6) Three commands and a promise: If you learn to: "Trust in the Lord with all your heart." If you practice: "Do not depend on your own understanding." If you are careful to: "Seek his will in all you do." God's promise is to: "direct your paths."

If worry is poison? Trust is God's antidote. The more we trust, the less we worry but how? Somehow, we stop depending on ourselves and learn to seek God's will.

We spend more time on our knees in prayer. Replacing worry with trust enables me to pray for my family without unduly interfering in their business. Replacing worry with trust permits me to work hard and leave the results to God. Replacing worry with trust strengthens my faith in the God who always loves me.

During a routine visit with an elderly member of the church, a minister noticed an empty chair by the bed and asked about it. The man replied, "I had a difficult time learning to pray. A friend suggested I place an empty chair in front of me and picture Jesus Christ sitting and having a conversation with me like an old and trusted friend. That chair has been with me ever since."

A few days later, the daughter called to tell the pastor her father died. "I was only out of the room for a minute. When I returned, he was gone. He looked so peaceful. Then I noticed something odd about his hand. It was resting on the chair - the empty chair."

It's been said that ulcers are caused not by what you eat, but by what is eating you! Are you being eaten alive by worries? Maybe you need to replace your rocking chair of human worries with a chair full of heavenly trust. When is the last time you had a conversation with Jesus? All it takes is a commitment to pray. Let's face it: a little bit of prayer sure beats a lot of worry.

Prayer Challenge: Pray today for God to help you replace worry with trust.

August 6 - Remembering Zig Ziglar

John 15:1-8

Before becoming a pastor, I took a business trip to Dallas, Texas. The purpose was to learn how to teach a motivational seminar designed by Zig Ziglar. While there, I was given a book: "Confessions of a Happy Christian." Zig's experiences touched my heart and dramatically changed my life. After staying up all night reading, crying, thinking, and praying, I gave my heart to Jesus Christ.

When Zig Ziglar died, I lost a friend and mentor. Many times, over the course of my life and career Zig offered encouragement. He signed the book that changed my life and added a verse from the Gospel of John that continues to guide me and my ministry today. "I am the vine; you are the branches. Those who remain in Me, and I in them, will produce much fruit." Zig also gave me a lapel pin with the symbol of a fish with the number 7. Zig designed the pin knowing people would ask: "What does this mean?"

Zig's answer: "The fish means I am a Christian. The 7 is a reminder to practice my faith 7 days a week." Zig knew this pin would provide an opportunity to talk about our faith in a nonthreatening way. I still wear the pin and I have given hundreds of them away. So, in addition to helping me, Zig also taught me how to share my faith with others.

Author, motivational speaker, super salesman, Sunday school teacher; Zig Ziglar epitomized his most famous saying: "You can have everything in life that you want if you just help enough other people find what they want." Here are a few Zig quotes:

- "Your attitude plus your aptitude determines your altitude."
- "The elevator to success is broken, but the stairs are always available."
- "Some people find fault as if there is a reward for it."
- "If you aim at nothing, you will hit it every time."
- "A lot of people quit looking for work as soon as they get a job."
- "If you have stinkin' thinkin', then you need a checkup from the neck up."

Zig fell down a flight of stairs and sustained a serious head injury. At eighty years of age, he lost much of his energy and vitality. Yet, amid everything, Zig maintained his enthusiasm for living. "Focus on what you can do, not what you can't," became his new mantra. Ziglar's final book written with the help of his daughter, Julie, documents his final years: "Embrace the Struggle: Living Life on Life's Terms." Even in his final years, Zig provided an example of how to deal with tragedy and how to live out your final days.

My life has been blessed over the years knowing Zig Ziglar. My prayer is to be the same kind of encourager and mentor for others Zig has been for me. I can still hear Zig saying to me and so many others: "Go as far as you can see, then you can see farther."

Prayer Challenge: Who has been an influence in your life? How can you thank them?

August 7 - Traveling

1 Peter 5:1-11

I don't travel well. Whether it is old age, lack of experience, or just being naïve I am aware that I do not possess the gift of travel common sense. This became evident while flying to Durbin, South Africa for a series of meetings. Great opportunity? Certainly. But first, I must get there. Sometimes, just getting there is part of the adventure.

Lesson One: Traveling is not the time to wing it. I was not well prepared. Passports, money exchange, international calling and boarding passes are all areas that leave no room to "figure it out as you go along." At our first stop I filled out a residence card and handed it to the customs agent. Simple enough. "I'm only there for nine hours," so I partially filled out the card. The customs officer threw a fit and marked every line I left blank and gave me a lecture. When I apologized and claimed inexperience, he replied: "Don't they teach yanks how to read?"

Lesson Two: Be polite, ask questions and smile. At the airport, there are many lines and lots of confusion. Flights were missed and tempers were flaring. It was tempting to express my own frustration but instead I complimented the agents' patience. He smiled, looked at my ticket and corrected an error that could cause problems later.

Lesson Three: Be open to opportunities. The first flight lasted eleven hours in seats jammed together. So, it seemed natural to talk to the lady squeezed in beside me. She was traveling to attend a funeral for her thirteen-year-old niece. I expressed my sympathy and introduced myself. She was startled and said, "your name is the same as mine, Davies." We talked about death and the difficulties of losing a young member of the family. I asked about the history of her name and heard an amazing story about slave families forced to take the name of their owner. Now her family was in Africa, England, America, and the Caribbean. We began as strangers and departed friends.

There is a song that reminds me of what it means to be a Christian whether in an airplane or witnessing to a neighbor. "I've got peace like a river. I've got peace like a river in my soul. I've got joy like a fountain in my soul. I've got faith like a mountain in my soul. I've got love like an ocean in my soul. I've got Christ as my Savior in my soul."

The opportunity to be a witness is all around us. While it's true that I have a lot to learn about travelling I am amazed at how God uses these times to teach valuable lessons and provide opportunities to witness my faith. Also, it's comforting to know God provides "peace like a river in my soul." One more lesson: I travelled 36 hours with no opportunity to shower, brush my teeth or shave. Next time, I'll bring a shaver and toothbrush in my carry-on bag, for the sake of my fellow passengers. It's the least I can do.

Prayer Challenge: How has God given you opportunities to witness your faith?

August 8 - A Diverse World

Matthew 5:3-10

Nearly 500 of us came from more than 50 countries to Durbin, South Africa. We met at a church, burrowed in the heart of the downtown sprawl, surrounded by street vendors and small businesses. From the outside, our church looked more like an office building but as soon as you walked in the door, you knew God was in this Holy place.

There was singing: loud, boisterous, and full of celebration. "San-na, san-na-ni-na, san-na, san-na, san-na." Over and over, we sang, first as they sing in South Africa, then English. "Holy, O holy Lord, great God of power and might." With the same music in the background, we prayed: "This is the day that you have made. Help us rejoice in it and be glad. Remind us of the privileges we enjoy as your people: to come to you in these moments, to confess our sins, to receive forgiveness and give it, to pray and sing and listen, to renew our fainting spirits, to rest in your promises. Open our eyes to see you. Open our ears to hear your Word. San-na, san-na-ni-na, san-na, san-na, san-na."

We heard the words of Jesus in other languages. "Blessed are the poor in spirit, for theirs is the kingdom of heaven. Blessed are those who mourn for they will be comforted. Blessed are the meek, for they will inherit the earth. Blessed are those who hunger and thirst for righteousness, for they will be filled. Blessed are the merciful, for they will receive mercy. Blessed are the pure in heart, for they will see God. Blessed are the peacemakers, for they will be called children of God. Blessed are those who are persecuted for righteousness' sake, for theirs is the kingdom of heaven." (Mat 5:3-10)

Hearing this familiar passage in several languages added new meaning and life to familiar words. The meeting was important but what I truly enjoyed was the opportunity to meet Christian leaders from all over the world and hear their amazing stories.

A missionary lived in East Germany within a few blocks of the wall. When it was torn down, she was afraid to go across for fear they would arrest her. A pastor from Poland described when she was first married, she had to appear early at a specified location and stand in line for over six hours to claim a washing machine. Ian from Australia, pastors three churches, plus administers much of the education efforts throughout Australia. An elderly pastor from South Africa described the horrors of apartheid and the amazing transformation that took place after Nelson Mandela became President.

Then, there were the prayers, the singing and the worship spoken in many languages but always full of energy and excitement. There were many cultures but, in the end, we became one – one in spirit, one in Jesus. Standing among my 500 new friends from all over the world, I learned we are all united in one faith, by one love, one Spirit; we are one people of God.

Prayer Challenge: Thank you for the lessons of other cultures and communities.

August 9 - Zulu

1 Thessalonians 4:9-12

Before entering a Zulu village, we walked a circular pathway surrounded by a wooden fence to end up at a gate. There we asked the guard for permission to enter. Until then, we were the enemy, and the villagers would fight to defend themselves. "Sanibona," (Hi.) we shouted to the warriors guarding the gate. We then asked for permission to enter. The warriors opened the gate, "Ngiyanemukela!" (Welcome!) As we entered, the guide said the key to being welcomed in a Zulu village was to seek to understand their customs and language. This was considered a sign of respect and common courtesy. We were taught new phrases. "Unjani." (How are you?) "Ngikhona." (I'm fine.)

My previous knowledge of anything Zulu came from old movies where natives were portrayed as simple and cruel savages. Entering this Zulu village in South Africa I was exposed to a culture rich with customs and traditions. I also learned more about the people who were portraying Zulu villagers. Our guide and many of the warriors and villagers were students at the university using their salary to finance their education.

The highlight of the tour was the dancing and singing which is an integral part of Zulu culture. Each dance symbolized something happening within the clan.

The rhythmic beating of the drums and the intricate movements tell a story. As we watched and listened, we began to appreciate the passion and energy of the Zulu culture.

Paul wrote: "Make it your goal to live a quiet life, minding your own business and working with your hands, just as we instructed you before. Then people who are not Christians will respect the way you live." (1 Thes. 4:11-12) Paul is teaching us how to be Christians in the everyday world where we live, eat, run errands, go to school and work. Every day, God gives opportunities to witness what we believe. These opportunities only come when each person or group can learn to show respect for the other.

Meeting a stranger is much like entering a Zulu village. You walk a path through a fence of suspicion to come to a gate guarded by lack of trust. You enter by asking permission and first seek to understand the customs and traditions of the person you meet. This is a sign of respect. As you listen to their story, those gates and barriers that once stood between you gradually come down. This is where God gives you opportunities. As you find common ground and share similar stories you cease being strangers and become friends. As friends, you share your hopes and dreams and eventually your faith story. God works within the bonds of friendship to sow seeds of love and grace.

We entered the Zulu village through a heavily guarded gate as strangers asking fierce warriors for permission to enter. We left through another gate with no fence, open and unguarded. We entered as potential enemies or strangers, but we left as friends. "Salani kahle Mngani." (Goodbye, friend.)

Prayer Challenge: Help me better understand the stories of people around me.

August 10 - Jerks

Luke 17:1-10

You are driving to work, minding your own business. Suddenly, someone runs a stop sign and with squealing tires, zips in front of your car, forcing you to slam on the brakes and swerve out of the way. You are a nervous wreck but the jerk in the other car never seems to acknowledge his mistake and speeds merrily down the highway.

How would you react? Would you scream, cry, shake your fist, curse him and his ancestry? Would you spend the rest of the morning describing what happened? Would your day be ruined because of the senseless, irrational, act of a stupid jerk who thinks the open road is paved for him? "Calm down, Larry!" Okay, okay, I'm calm.

Yet, the other driver -- the jerk who caused your suffering is happily going on with life having no knowledge of what he did to you. Think about it. The other driver was responsible for the near accident, but your reaction was not his fault. The real damage done to you was entirely self-inflicted. In a word, it is called: resentment.

One definition of resentment is to re-feel the pain. Resentment is like accidentally cutting your hand with a knife and then deciding to avenge yourself by stabbing the other hand. Ouch, that hurts! Jesus said: "If your brother sins, rebuke him and if he repents, forgive him. If he sins against you seven times in a day and seven times comes back to you and says, 'I repent,' forgive him." (Luke 17:3,4)

Does this mean we have to forgive the jerk that tried to run over us? Jesus also said: "If you have faith as small as a mustard seed, you can say to this mulberry tree, 'Be uprooted and planted in the sea,' and it will obey you." (Luke 17:6) The mulberry tree has extensive roots that run deep into the soil. It's nearly impossible to uproot. Resentment has extensive roots that run deep within our soul. Forgiveness is a process that begins as a tiny mustard seed. As the mustard seed of forgiveness grows the roots of resentment, like the mulberry tree, are loosened and our faith is strengthened.

Does this kind of forgiveness sound impossible? Sure, without God. Yet, one psychiatrist wrote that 75% of his patients could walk out of treatment if they understood what it means to forgive and be forgiven. Such is the power of grace. "Christianity doesn't often lessen suffering. What it does is enable you to take it, to face it, to work through it and eventually to convert it." Terry Waite

Does an attitude of forgiveness ever come easy? Never! It's a process that we must work at continually, but God makes a clear promise that your willingness to forgive will give you a faith that will move mountains and change your life. Great! Now if I can only forgive that jerk on the highway that almost killed me!

Prayer Challenge: Who do you need to forgive? Who should you ask to forgive you?

August 11 - Punishment

Matthew chapter 23

A man was standing at a busy intersection wearing a sign: "I cheated. This is my punishment." When interviewed he said, "I'm wearing the sign as punishment for being unfaithful." He added: "I thought she was kidding." After a pause, he hung his head and said: "She wasn't kidding! In order to make things right, I have to do whatever is necessary." This man's wife was angry, likely for a good reason.

In chapter 23 of Matthew, Jesus was angry. Some people always look and act angry, so we don't pay much attention but when a person like Jesus who is known for being loving and compassionate becomes angry, you notice. Why was Jesus angry? Also, why was he so angry at Pharisees who are reputed to be good community leaders? Answer? Because they too cheated: They were unfaithful to their calling before God.

Seven times in Matthew 23, Jesus proclaimed: "How terrible it will be for you." We do everything for show. We are quick to condemn and slow to praise. We place higher priority on serving ourselves before serving God. Our word is no longer sacred. We major in the minors and miss what is important. We are clean on the outside but inside we are filthy. We look good on the outside but inside we are dead.

How did the Pharisees, our religious leaders respond? Jesus was arrested, whipped, beaten, and cruelly murdered on a cross. How should we respond? Stand on a street with a sign? "I cheated on God! This is my punishment!" Is that what Jesus wants?

Jesus cries out: "O Jerusalem, Jerusalem, the city that kills the prophets and stones God's messengers! How often I have wanted to gather your children together as a hen protects her chicks beneath her wings, but you wouldn't let me." (Mat. 23:37)

"You kill the prophets." God looks for courage not cover-ups. "How I wanted to gather your children." We deserve judgement but we are offered grace. "But you wouldn't let me." An unwillingness to confess is worse than the sin itself because you deny God the opportunity to be a loving parent and protect you beneath his wings. Refuse to confess and you reject a loving God who longs to forgive and restore you.

Imagine Jesus with tears in his eyes describing a mother hen shielding her chicks beneath her wings. God longs to comfort, protect and restore you. The alternative is to refuse to confess, reject God's love offering and face emptiness and isolation.

We can be restored and renewed. It sure beats the alternative: Standing on a street corner with a sign proclaiming to all: "I cheated on God. This is my punishment." We are given the opportunity to join the rest of our fellow sinners in celebration of the One who can restore us. Christ has died. Christ is risen. Christ will come again.

Prayer Challenge: Take a moment and imagine Jesus shielding you with his wings.

August 12 - Reaching Our Youth

2 Timothy 2: 1-2

Several leaders gathered to talk about how churches could more closely work together in reaching youth in our community. The person who asked for the meeting spoke of attending churches where there were virtually no children or youth and no interest in being a church for them. Yet nearly every church in his community declined over the last four years and may continue to decline if something doesn't change.

We quickly agreed that churches could no longer start youth groups by simply hiring a college student, offering pizza, an evening of fun and possibly a Bible study. Many of our youth are already overwhelmed with choices as to how to spend their time.

One youth leader spoke of spending time at the local middle school, volunteering and speaking to several of the groups. He often ate lunch in the cafeteria and spent time getting to know the students. He spoke of the need for students to have a responsible adult to relate to. Another person spoke of the importance of mission experiences where youth and adults traveled together to help people in need. There was a bond formed among youth and adults that changed their perspective about ministry and the church.

Another leader summed it up: "Our youth yearn for one-on-one spiritual relationships with adults. We need more committed adults willing to spend quality time invested in relating to our youth. Youth ministry starts with the pastor and is modeled by adults throughout the church. Youth leaders should spend as much time teaching adult volunteers as they do interacting with the youth themselves."

In the Bible, Paul said much the same thing to a young pastor named Timothy: "Be strong through the grace that God gives you in Christ Jesus. You have heard me teach things that have been confirmed by many reliable witnesses. Now teach these truths to other trustworthy people who will be able to pass them on to others." (2 Timothy 2:1-2)

Teach people who will pass them on to others. Simple enough, or is it? The world has dramatically changed since 1960. Yet the mission of our church has not changed. If there is going to be a viable ministry to our youth, adults must take an active interest. Successful youth ministry begins with a pastor who personally models the importance of teaching the truth to others and then helps to train adults to become more involved.

This is where I realized that the first person who needed to change was me. I too must display a more active interest in youth ministry and model what it means to teach the truth to others. I must practice what I preach. So, I bought several bags of toiletry items. Why? One of our leaders mentioned their youth group giving away toiletries and food to the homeless in a local park every Sunday afternoon. This Sunday, I will join them.

Prayer Challenge: How can you be a part of modeling teaching the truth?

August 13 - Clutter

2 Corinthians 11:1-6

I received an email from a relative: "We've never had a chance to visit your church, so I checked it out online. Your sanctuary is beautiful, but have you seen the picture of your office?" Now, I was curious. "Maybe you should take a peek." She included the link and when I clicked on it, there was what could only be described as – ground zero of a nuclear blast or extreme clutter or disaster area or site condemned! Papers strewn all over my desk. You could hardly see my computer. A lamp shade tilted. Pictures, books, and mementos scattered all about.

I was embarrassed, ashamed and humiliated. I knew something needed to be done, but deep down I knew it wouldn't be right to eliminate my relative. Would it? (Okay Larry, get serious.) There was no way around it. Something needed to be done.

"With tongue planted firmly in cheek," Chuck Swindoll shared steps toward achieving a cluttered mind. "Say yes, every time someone asks you to do something. Don't plan any time for leisure and rejuvenation. Don't be satisfied with your accomplishments - keep moving. Acquire all the latest technology so you can simplify your life."

Guilty. Guilty! Guilty!! In addition to having a cluttered office, I say yes far too often. I plan very little time for leisure and rejuvenation. I am seldom satisfied with my accomplishments. I've often acquired the latest technology hoping for a simpler life only to find myself maintaining yet another gadget. I confess! I am guilty of a cluttered mind and a cluttered life.

Many of us feel the stress of a hectic, cluttered lifestyle. Paul wrote in 2 Corinthians: "I fear that somehow you will be led away from your pure and simple devotion to Christ, just as Eve was deceived by the serpent. You seem to believe whatever anyone tells you..." (11:3) When our lives are cluttered, we can be led astray.

Ella Wheeler Wilcox wrote a beautiful poem that begins: "One ship drives east and another drives west with the selfsame winds that blow: 'Tis the set of the sails and not the gales, which tells us the way to go." Two ships driven by the wind, yet one stays on course. Are you sailing where you desire or caught in the gales of a cluttered lifestyle? The answer is found in the word: simplify. We must learn to simplify our lives. The reward is a less complicated life, not more and the fruit is the opportunity to enjoy a long-lasting, satisfying, rewarding, intimate relationship with almighty God.

Next: "I want to get rid of the clutter in my office and my life -- but how?"

August 14 - Clutter – Conclusion

Mark 4:1-20

I am guilty of a complicated, cluttered life. Ella Wheeler Wilcox: "One ship drives east and another drives west, with the selfsame winds that blow: 'Tis the set of the sails and not the gales which tell us the way to go." Two ships driven by the wind, yet one stays on course. Why? How? Ella continues: "Like the winds of the sea are the ways of fate, as we voyage along through life: 'Tis the set of the soul that decides its goal and not the calm or the strife." I was caught in the gales of a cluttered lifestyle. My answer? Simplify.

Simplifying started in my office. I filled trash cans with unused books, old gifts, and files. Anything not needed, including furniture, was given away or thrown away. People walking by looked in with a worried expression and asked, "Are you moving?"

So, what's next? In the parable of the farmer sowing seeds Jesus talks about the seed growing in thorny ground: "The thorny ground represents those who hear and accept the Good News but all too quickly the message is crowded out by the cares of this life, the lure of wealth and the desire for nice things so no crop is produced." (Mark 4:18-19)

Jesus is describing a cluttered lifestyle. Chuck Swindoll provides a good checklist: "Do you say 'no' enough to keep from being overly committed? Do you maintain a good balance between work and leisure time? Do you enjoy appropriate satisfaction in your accomplishments? Does technology simplify your life rather than complicate it?"

Max Lucado wrote about a farmer who complained about the lake on his property always needing to be stocked and managed. The hills ruined his roads and added wear and tear to his vehicle. The cattle needed constant care with fencing and feeding. What a headache. He decided to sell the place and move somewhere else. He called a real estate agent and made plans to list the farm. Then he read the ad: "A lovely farm in an ideal location – quiet and peaceful, contoured with rolling hills, carpeted with soft meadows, nourished by a fresh lake and blessed with well-bred livestock." After reading the ad several times, he called the realtor and said, "I'm sorry. I've changed my mind. I'm not going to sell. I've been looking for a place like this all my life."

Maybe the farmer discovered the alternative to a cluttered lifestyle. Paul wrote: "I have learned how to be content whether I have much or little." (Philippians 4:11) Maybe the real secret to a simplified life is in learning how to be content with much or with little.

I now have a less cluttered office and hopefully a less cluttered lifestyle. I still struggle with saying 'no' occasionally and maintaining a good balance between work and leisure but I'm doing better. But please, no more pictures of my office!

Prayer Challenge: Lord, guide me toward simplifying my lifestyle.

August 15 - Arnold Palmer

Luke 14: 1-24

I don't want to brag, (Yes, I do!) but I played eighteen holes of golf with Arnold Palmer and won by three strokes! No, he was not a golf klutz with the same name. No, I did not cheat. No, I can't afford to bribe him! Yes, his health was good at the time! We played in Hilton Head Island, South Carolina on a beautiful golf course full of hazards and traps.

Arnie was kind but he was also determined. For the first 13 holes it was nip and tuck as we struggled to a tie score. He would win one hole with a spectacular birdie then I would win another. But on the 14th hole, I sunk a 35-foot putt to go ahead by one stroke. On the 17th hole, I made another birdie. And finally on the 18th, Arnie went for broke on a long putt and missed. Victory was mine. Let the celebration begin!

"Yahoo! I beat Arnie!" I shouted while pumping fists into the air and performing a version of the funky chicken! (Wouldn't you like to see that?) Are you tired of my arrogant boasting yet? Of course, you are. But here is the point. When you hear someone sound-off like this? Do you have an urge to hug him, or do you want to chastise her? No one enjoys the company of a bragger or a namedropper.

Jesus said: "If you are invited to a wedding feast, don't head for the best seat. What if someone more respected has also been invited? The host will say, 'Let this person sit here instead.' Then you will be embarrassed and will have to take whatever seat is left at the foot of the table! "Do this instead— sit at the foot of the table. For the proud will be humbled, but the humble will be honored." (parts of Luke14: 8-11)

Jesus is talking about more than good table manners, isn't he? The most important people at a wedding are the bride and groom. Not you! By maneuvering to get the best seat you detract from the couple's happy moment and look like an insensitive jerk or worse. We see it in others, but do we notice it in ourselves? Not always.

By trying so hard to beat Arnold Palmer, I missed the opportunity to enjoy his company. Likewise, our arrogant attitude detracts from the God we all claim to serve and prevents us from appreciating and learning from the immensely talented people who surround us. Our society applauds a "win at any cost" mentality and expects us to revel in victory. Yet, Jesus clearly demonstrates another answer. It is in our humility not our boasting that we truly discover God.

Now Larry, what is the truth about that golf match? (Pause) It is amazing what computers can do? They simulate almost anything, even a game of golf. Yes, I did play Arnold Palmer at Hilton Head, but from the comfort of my computer screen. So, all in one story, I've been exposed as arrogant, boasting and slightly deceitful. Maybe this is why we need God and from the sound of my bragging? I need Him too.

Prayer Challenge: Lord, help me focus on you and others and less on myself.

August 16 - Integrity

Psalm 15

The ancient Chinese built the "Great Wall" which stretches for several thousand miles, to ensure their security from foreign invaders. Yet during the first hundred years after the wall was completed, China was successfully invaded three times, not by going over the wall or tearing it down, but by bribing the guards and simply marching through the gates. China spent years building the "Great Wall" but didn't spend enough time building the character of the gatekeepers.

David wrote Psalm 15 to set standards that would define our integrity as people of God. He asks: "Who may worship in your sanctuary, Lord? Who may enter your presence on your holy hill?" In other words, "What do you expect of us?"

1. *Those who lead blameless lives...* Do we live out what we believe?
2. *...and do what is right...* our day-to-day habits and choices.
3. *...speaking the truth from sincere hearts.* Do we mean what we say?
4. *Those who refuse to slander others...* no gossip or spreading rumors.
5. *...or harm nor speak evil of friends...* we treat people with respect.

A Daily Dose of Godly Encouragement: Medicine for Tough Days

6. *Those who despise persistent sinners...* Who is influencing whom?
7. *...and honor faithful followers...* We become like the people we hang with.
8. *...and keep their promises...* We do what we say.
9. *...do not charge interest...* help a friend in need: generously and unselfishly.
10. *...who refuse to accept a bribe.* We do not corrupt our conduct, ever.

Ten standards to guide our integrity. Can you do all of them? Of course not! That is why you and I need God and why we need to be in church. We do our best and trust in God for the rest. Psalm 15 ends with this promise: *"Such people will stand firm forever."*

A preacher once gave a sermon on honesty. The next day, she took the bus into town and after taking a seat, noticed she was given too much change. She tried to convince herself that the extra money was a gift from God but knew better. Before getting off the bus she handed the driver the extra money and said: "You made a mistake and gave me too much change?"

"That was no mistake," said the driver. "I was in your church yesterday and heard your sermon on honesty. So, this morning, I gave you a little test!"

People are watching. What will they see in you?

Prayer Challenge: Lord, help me live a life of integrity and kindness.

August 17 - "Think of Me:" Remembering David

Psalm 121

When you hear the crack of bat and ball, or hear the umpire bellow out his call of "safe" or "out" When you see a ball in lofted flight, or players tangled in the night as runner slides and baseman tags -- think of me. (Poem by Rev. Richard A. Barclay)

Four baseball players returning from church camp to play in an all-star game. One of them, sixteen-year-old David, was sitting in the back seat. David's mother was waiting at the ballfield. A man ran a stop sign and rammed into the side of the players' car. Three boys were injured. David died on the way to the hospital.

When class bells ring and hallways crowd with endless chatter soft and loud of ordered chaos -- When wanton mischief calls and laughter causes sides to split and tears to fall as mirthful mouths grow wide in glee -- think of me.

David was the son of our organist and grew up in our church. He played with my daughter and occasionally acted up during worship. But it was David who asked good questions about God and showed a desire to grow stronger in his faith. He had a knack for making friends. David was a talented ball player and a typical teenager who played his music loud and moved fast. In other words, David was normal which is why his death was so difficult. David should not have died. Once again, we are cruelly reminded how life isn't fair and tragedies happen.

When music rocks and speakers boom compelling all within the room to echo lyrics that rap the soul -- think of me. When hands are held and friends embrace with words of comfort, love and grace to shoulder sorrow and share in joys -- think of me.

Tragedies remind us why we need God. I could not write these words if I didn't passionately believe David is safely with God. But now what? When tragedy strikes, how do we respond? How do we go on and keep David's memory alive?

When prayer is short and words too mute to speak the pain that's taken root deep within the spirit's womb, then -- think of me.

God provided comfort when the community surrounded David's family. There was comfort when two churches opened their doors to accommodate the large crowd of mourners. There was comfort when fellow teachers reached out to David's mother. There was comfort when David McCraw's teammates came in uniform to pay their respects and carry his coffin to a final resting-place. Maybe, this is what being a Christian is about: Offering comfort, learning lessons, and hopefully, growing stronger in our faith. Then, David's death will not be in vain.

Think of me for I am there in every place and face and heart that beats and every breath that's drawn in life, not death; my strength, my love, my joy to give, for as you go on, so shall I live in you, as I also live in God. (Rev. Richard A. Barclay)

Prayer Challenge: In the midst of tragedy, how does God provide comfort?

August 18 - A Key Mystery

Matthew 5:21-26

While shopping with Mell, I reached for my keys and to my surprise, pulled out two rings full of keys. Unfortunately, I only owned one. How did an extra set of keys end up in my pocket? Who did they belong to? Did I grab them, thinking they were mine? Am I a secret kleptomaniac taking what doesn't belong to me? I had no clue. However, someone was missing a set of keys who was likely trapped without a car.

Quickly, we retraced our steps to places visited and asked if anyone had lost their keys. No one recognized the keys or knew of anyone stranded. I discovered a panic button on the key, so for several minutes we drove around the parking lots, hitting the button. No car horns, no flashing lights. Nothing! Someone was frantically looking for their keys. I inconvenienced someone and no matter how hard I tried; I could not rectify my mistake.

Have you ever hurt someone intentionally or unintentionally? Made a mistake that cost somebody else? Said something that hurt someone's feelings? Sure, you have. Haven't we all? The real question is: "What do we do about it?" Jesus addressed this very issue. He said, "If you bring your gift to the altar and remember your brother has something against you, leave your gift and be reconciled. Then offer your gift." (Matthew 5:23-24)

We all make mistakes. We hurt other people and they hurt us. The lesson: Leave everything behind and seek reconciliation. I had someone else's keys in my pocket, and I could not go home until I found the owner and corrected my mistake.

My wife started looking through the discount cards on the mystery key ring. One card was for a store in the shopping center we were in. A store where we thought I might have picked up the keys. "Honey," she said. "Why don't you ask customer service to check out the owner of this discount card?" Sure enough, customer service scanned the card and identified the owner. Within a few moments they were on the phone notifying the owner of her missing keys.

Whew! I could finally go home. If only, all our mistakes could be so easily resolved. But, I learned an important lesson. We make mistakes. We hurt people and we are hurt. Jesus says, no matter what the mistake or hurt. We must do our best to be reconciled.

I know about several occasions where I failed to seek reconciliation and on other occasions, I was the one hurt. I too must do better at being reconciled. To forgive and be forgiven is a critical part of our witness as a follower of Jesus.

Just one nagging question: How did those keys end up in my pocket? Sigh!

Prayer Challenge: Who hurt you? Who have you hurt? How can you be reconciled?

August 19 - Wild Weddings

First Corinthians chapter 13

As a minister, I do weddings, lots of weddings. Most of them are problem-free, predictable ceremonies of worship providing precious memories and pictures for everyone. Over the years, however, I have been involved in a few weddings which can only be classified as: "Wild!"

One "wild" wedding took place between bands performing at a Blue Grass Festival. (Yes, you heard me right!) The groom dreamed of being married as a part of the festival but could not find a woman crazy enough to marry him under those circumstances. His lifelong wish finally came true, and we all gathered on stage in between acts as the girl of his dreams said yes while the crowd hooted and cheered. After the ceremony, there was a standing ovation for the happy couple. I was tempted to turn and bow but restrained myself.

At another "wild" wedding, I asked for the rings and the best man handed me a pink, plastic "Crackerjacks" special. *"This is a cheap looking ring! Is this how the marriage is going to go?"* I dramatically asked and everyone laughed, except my wife who thought I lost my mind. The rings were replaced, and the rest of the ceremony went off without a hitch until the couple strolled down the aisle and the groom sprayed his family in bright green and yellow string.

But the prize goes to a couple who each wrote silly vows as a surprise for their mate. First, the bride asked me to read an additional set of marriage vows she wrote for her husband. Then, just before the service, the groom pulled me aside and handed me another set of vows also to be read as a surprise to his new wife.

As instructed, I turned to the husband and asked him to gaze lovingly upon his wife and respond to the following with: "I agree!" Do you agree to cook steak and potatoes every Friday? Do you agree to cut the grass and take out the trash? Do you agree to keep the cars clean? Do you agree to have coffee ready when I wake up? Do you agree to take me shopping once a week without complaining?

My next instructions were to have the bride take the groom by the hand, look lovingly into his eyes and repeat the vows written for her: I agree to lovingly serve you breakfast in bed every Saturday morning and to learn how to bake homemade pies and cobblers. I will also "never" insist that you go shopping with me for more than one hour at a time.

Afterwards, I commented: "This couple doesn't need a minister. They need a lawyer to pick his way through these vows." A proper ending might have been to declare them both insane. But after laughing, I discovered an important lesson.

Solomon, said: "There is a time for everything: a time to weep and a time to laugh, a time to mourn and a time to dance." (Ecclesiastes 3:4) Life is short and God reminds us to make the most of it: to keep our priorities in place.

You have to admire a couple secure enough in their love for each other; they can play a practical joke in the midst of such a serious commitment. Assuming they can hold on to their ability to laugh and poke fun at each other, there is hope for a long-lasting, long-loving marriage. Let's face it; with a better sense of humor, there would be more hope and a better future for us all.

Prayer Challenge: Read 1 Corinthians 13 and reflect on the meaning of "Love."

August 20 - Suitcases & Stress

Matthew 6:25-34

Here is a way to have fun! Line up ten suitcases and attempt to carry them. "Let's see, I jam this one under my arm. This one on top of my head and this one goes between my legs!" I attempted this interesting but stupid feat at a church service and succeeded in picking up nine suitcases (or was it eight) but as I swung the last one over my shoulder, the rest of my body followed, and I was lying amidst a heap of luggage on the floor.

Now what? I cannot carry but so many suitcases without falling. So, sheepishly, I asked for help. Immediately someone picked up four or five of the suitcases while I retrieved the others and in just a few moments we easily accomplished together what I could not do alone. Once I asked for help, an impossible task became manageable. The stress and burdens of daily life can be compared to juggling too many suitcases. We can carry two or three, maybe six or seven but as burdens increase, our capacity to carry the load diminishes. Eventually, we must ask for help.

Example? A grieving family prepares for life without a loved one. Students finishing end-of-semester papers and exams. Single parents facing too many bills, too many needs and too little income. Day-to-day pressures of cooking, cleaning, child rearing, work-related problems, health issues and the list goes on and the suitcases multiply.

The stress and burdens continue to lie heavily upon our sagging shoulders year after year eventually causing us to stumble, fall and lie helplessly among the pile. No matter how strong you may be, the load cannot be carried alone. It is impossible!

Jesus said: "Don't worry about everyday life—whether you have enough food, drink, and clothes. Doesn't life consist of more than food and clothing? Look at the birds. They don't need to plant or harvest or put food in barns because your heavenly father feeds them. And you are far more valuable to him than they are. Can all your worries add a single moment to your life? Of course not. You have so little faith." (Matthew 6:25-26)

This is more than a simplistic "do not worry" speech. We are reminded: Replace worry with faith. Go back to the basics of working on your relationship with God. Spend more time in prayer. Share your burdens with a trusted friend. Faith will eventually lead to trust in a God who will lovingly guide you during difficult times. Take a quiet moment to sit and read a devotion. Be content with looking for God's help today. Tomorrow will bring its own worries. Attend worship at a local church. Become involved.

Your faith can provide needed help turning impossible tasks into manageable ones. No matter what stress or burdens you may be facing, there is help available, if you are willing to ask. Replace your worries with faith and let God help you carry the load. Now, if only someone would help me get these suitcases back to my house!

Prayer Challenge: How many suitcases are you carrying? Replace worries with faith.

August 21 - Blockbuster Video

Colossians 3:1-17

Movies played an important role in my life. I grew up in rural Arkansas where they had only one movie theater. It wasn't unusual for me to spend most any Saturday catching the latest double feature. I learned to appreciate history watching, "Longest Day." When walking by groups of birds or going to the beach I still remember, "The Birds" and "Jaws." There were the date flicks: "Romeo and Juliet" and "Love Story." Even my young faith was partially shaped by "Godspell" and "Jesus Christ Superstar."

As a young adult, I eagerly purchased a VCR. Not long afterward movie rentals caught on and became ingrained as part of our culture. Bad weather sent more parents to buy videos than groceries. I became a regular customer at Blockbuster Video often driving 30 miles out of my way. What happened to Blockbuster? Did people stop watching movies? Of course not, but the way we watched movies changed from Beta & VHS tapes to DVD to watching online. Blockbuster was slow to recognize and adapt to the changes, dwindled in size, and eventually declared bankruptcy.

For centuries, the place to learn about God and live out your faith was within a local church. But fewer and fewer people now consider church to be an important part of their life. It doesn't help that church leaders within my denomination and others have been arguing for years over how to deal with issues related to human sexuality. Over a quarter of our United Methodist churches have broken away in frustration. While church leaders argue, people in the pews have increasingly walked away or stopped attending.

Could the church be on a path like Blockbuster Video? Probably not but I do believe this story is a warning. Has the church been slow to adapt to the spiritual needs of a changing culture? Like Blockbuster, have we responded with too little, too late?

Readers respond: "My daughter believes in a power greater than us but cannot bring herself to believe in God. We, as a church, have not answered this perspective at all. We have a message as Christians, but we fail to communicate it in modern terminology young people can grasp. Christian music helps but we need more." – Debbie

"I don't think I am alone in struggling to find connectedness at church. We do a poor job with 'singles.' I tried to join the 'young adult' ministry at my church. We coordinated an outing and wound up sharing the church van with the 'seniors' group. This is the sort of stuff that happens. I like people. I simply want to feel 'connected.' - Deanna

"Many people are too 'self-centered.' Everything is about us and our needs. We need to be more focused on others. What do others see when they look at us? Do they see a caring Christian who cares about them, or someone who goes to church on Sunday, and it stops there? Has church become just another social club?" – Sharon

These heartfelt letters help us understand three problem areas within the church: We don't communicate well with those who struggle. We are not helping to connect those who feel disconnected from the church. We appear self-centered and do not reflect the love of Christ in conversation and action.

Next: A Retreat Center

August 22 - Blockbuster Video and The Church

Hebrews chapter 13

Richmond Hill is a retreat center located on a hill overlooking downtown Richmond, Virginia. According to the brochure, the Sisters of the Visitation of Monte Maria came to Richmond in 1866 at the end of the Civil War to pray for the healing of the city. They moved into two of the city's older mansions and turned them into a place of prayer. You can still join the community three times a day for prayer and worship.

I was there along with other ministers for a retreat where we worshipped with the Richmond Hill community. The services were simple and contained long sometimes uncomfortable periods of silence. But there was something extraordinary about the setting. You could feel the presence of God within every part of the building. I came away from the retreat center feeling refreshed and thankful.

During a break, I found a quiet place to read a daily devotion stored in my Kindle. One statement from a favorite author was especially meaningful. I typed the quote on my smartphone and posted it on Facebook. At the same time, I received an email from someone requesting prayer. After replying, I forwarded the email to my prayer network.

Stop. Wait a minute. Isn't something wrong with this picture? I described a beautiful experience of worship and prayer but then, I'm reading eBooks, posting on Facebook and sending emails everywhere?

At the retreat center, I experienced the timeless basics of our faith. We pray. We worship. We fellowship. We encourage. We grow. We witness. We serve. The future of the church depends upon teaching and living out those fundamentals. At the same time, we learn to communicate with those who feel disconnected using every tool at our disposal whether through music, Bible study, worship, email, prayer networks or the social media. More importantly, we do everything reflecting the love and grace of Jesus Christ in our conversation and action.

The author of Hebrews writes: "Remember your leaders who taught you the word of God. Think of all the good that has come from their lives and follow the example of their faith. Jesus Christ is the same yesterday, today, and forever." (Heb 13:7-8) Remember your leaders. Follow their example. Jesus is the same yesterday, today and forever.

When the Sisters of the Visitation of Monte Maria came to Richmond, they established a church in the midst of a suffering city. Years later, we learn from their example. Prayer, worship, fellowship, encouragement, growth, witness, and service still matter whether in a monastery or posting on Facebook. "Jesus is the same yesterday, today and forever.

Next: Answers

August 23 - Blockbuster Video & the Church - Answers

Colossians 3:1-17

"Crystal Cathedral Bankrupt!" Citing debts of more than $43 million, the organization declares bankruptcy in a collapse blamed by some on its inability to keep up with the times. Sound familiar? This series started with an article about Blockbuster Video also slow to adapt. Have our churches been slow to adapt to a changing culture? Like the Crystal Cathedral and Blockbuster, have we responded with too little, too late?

Three problems were mentioned in letters: We don't communicate well with those who struggle. We are not helping to connect those who feel disconnected from the church. We appear self-centered and do not reflect the love of Christ in conversation and action.

At a retreat center, I experienced the timeless basics of our faith. The future of the church depends upon remembering, teaching, and living out the basics of our faith while at the same time learning to communicate with those who feel disconnected.

Paul wrote in Colossians: "Since God chose you to be the holy people he loves, you must clothe yourselves with tenderhearted mercy, kindness, humility, gentleness, and patience. Make allowance for each other's faults and forgive anyone who offends you. Remember, the Lord forgave you, so you must forgive others. Above all, clothe yourselves with love, which binds us all together in perfect harmony. And let the peace that comes from Christ rule in your hearts. For as members of one body, you are called to live in peace and always be thankful." (Col. 3:12-15)

We are chosen by God to be holy people, so we clothe ourselves with tenderhearted mercy, kindness, humility, gentleness, and patience and make allowance for each other's faults. Let peace from Christ rule in our hearts.

How is this lived out? "I went through a divorce and started to attend church again, but I felt so much guilt. So, it was a big step to walk into your church. I was welcomed by everyone, and I loved the service and teaching. I just want to thank you for creating such a warm and loving environment for people to hear the message, knowing that whatever level they're coming in at is okay – they'll be loved for who they are!" – Jim

"Your articles made me think about my church and our struggle. However, there is something missing that I think our church addresses and that's a corrective action block. Recently, a congregational study pulled us all together and helped us better understand our purpose. We prayed for each other and our church. Every gathering started with lighting a Christ candle to invoke His presence. That simple exercise carries forth today in almost every church meeting. It became the norm to ask for prayer requests in any church gathering. Prayer has changed us and our church. We make better choices now because we turn to God for help." - Liz

Yes, times are changing -- rapidly. Churches and businesses go bankrupt. But the basics of our faith never change: We pray. We worship. We fellowship. We encourage. We grow. We witness. We serve. We are chosen by God to be holy people, so we clothe ourselves with tenderhearted mercy, kindness, humility, gentleness, and patience and make allowance for each other's faults. Let peace from Christ rule in our hearts.

Prayer Challenge: How should you and your church respond to change?

August 24 - Help: I Can't Control My Dog!

Hebrews chapter 12

Our little cocker spaniel, Molly, was getting out of control. Her vet informed us that she may be dying. "She'll be craving water and food." He solemnly informed us. "Give her what she wants and make her comfortable." The doctor was too kind. Molly doesn't just crave food and water... she CRAVES food and water through the night.

At first, we were eager to do whatever Molly wanted because we felt sorry for her but after several months, Molly's condition improved. There is only one problem. She still wants food and water all through the night. She's crazy and driving me nuts.

Molly goes through the same routine every night. First, she gently pads over to our bed, sits down near my head and stares at me. (Why is it always me? Don't answer that.) Those penetrating eyes send lightning bolts through my dream world. Startled, I wake up and there sits Molly with a look of desperation as if she just completed a hot march across the desert. "Feed me! Now!"

After a while, I learned to sleep through the stare, so she learned a new tactic: heavy breathing. Molly would rise on her hind legs and place her snout directly in front of my face and begin to pant. When that stopped working, she began to whimper and then whine. Finally, Molly began barking, soft at first but building in intensity. Whenever Molly wants something; she barks. If we go to bed and leave her in my study? She barks. Go outside? Molly barks. Won't somebody help me? My dog is out of control!

A friend suggested I whip her into shape. "A good spanking never hurt anyone," he said. Another implied that I didn't understand her. After all, Molly is traumatized. A neighbor wanted Molly to come to her house. After all, dad never treated her right anyway. A minister suggested I pray over her. A psychiatrist recommended Ritalin. A lawyer wanted me to sue the kennel where we purchased her.

Whether you are teaching children or pets, everyone likes to give advice but whose advice do you follow? For a more reliable source I began looking through scripture. "For the Lord disciplines those he loves, and he punishes those he accepts as his children. As you endure this divine discipline, remember that God is treating you as his children. Whoever heard of a child who was never disciplined?" (Hebrews 12:6-7)

For God, discipline is an expression of love. Taking time to discipline is a clear indication of how much you care. By taking the time to consistently teach Molly when it is not okay to bark, I am showing her how much I love her. Your willingness to establish guidelines and expectations is a way of demonstrating love and establishing value as members of your family. The courage to discipline is a beautiful gift of love. Now if I can only teach Molly to let me sleep!

Prayer Challenge: God, help me lovingly understand and apply discipline.

August 25 - Vital Congregation

John 15:1-8

What does it mean to be a Vital Congregation? Does a vital congregation imply lots of people or programs? Can smaller churches be vital too? Recently, I attended a dedication service for a new education wing at a church in Virginia. Over the years, thanks to the leadership of their pastor and a dedicated group of church members, this little church has become a vital and growing congregation.

Sherriff Mike Miller works part-time as pastor and works full time as sheriff in a nearby county. He was asked to describe his church and what they are doing. "We are in an area both aging and rural, filled with farmers and other workers. Our community suffered due to the economic downturn. There is a need for basic supplies such as food. Elderly neighbors have basic housing needs. There is a growing homeless and substance abuse population. Higher gas prices are impacting everyone. Basics such as medication and utility expenses are becoming more expensive and out of the reach of many, especially the elderly and poor."

"Our congregation is attentive to individual acts of piety and acts of mercy. Acts of piety for us involve regularly attending worship, studying the scriptures, prayer, participating in the taking of sacraments, and sharing our faith with others. Acts of mercy include visiting the sick, feeding the hungry and collecting necessities for community needs. We try to find ways to love anyone who seeks our assistance. If our church no longer existed, our community would suffer by not receiving food, financial assistance, and spiritual growth opportunities. We promise to continue to grow in faith and then share that faith with others by feeding the hungry, helping the needy and providing spiritual growth opportunities to our church and the community."

Rev. Miller added: "No one is perfect and that's the way Jesus wants us. Jesus went to the streets to find the sick, the lame and the sinners. Jesus was there for the ones who come up short, who make mistakes, who are not perfect. A beautiful example of that is at the prayer and altar rail. Three of the posts that support this rail are upside down. Somehow the person who put the altar rail together made a mistake… or did he? I like to think that he deliberately placed these posts upside down as a reminder to us that we come to Jesus as imperfect, flawed people. When we come to this altar rail we find healing, forgiveness, and grace. We discover the true meaning of family, God's family."

What does it mean to be a vital congregation? It's not about size or programming, Jesus said: "You will know them by their fruit." (Mat. 7:16) Rev. Mike Miller and the church he serves certainly understands what it means to produce fruit for Jesus.

Prayer Challenge: How is God leading you to be more involved in your community?

August 26 - Elvis

Matthew 5:13-16

Occasionally, I act a little crazy. One year, the bulletin had a picture of Elvis Presley on the cover and the title: "Elvis in Concert: Rock & Roll Worship!" One person looked at the bulletin and sniffed, "Larry has lost his mind." Charles Wade wrote: "Elvis had an abiding love of gospel music. For him it was not affectation, nor a passing fancy. He returned to this part of his music repeatedly." Peter Guralnick wrote, "It is a story of celebrity and its consequences. It is, I think, a tragedy."

The worship service resembled an Elvis concert. "Just a Closer Walk with Thee" by our bells, "Crying in the Chapel and "Precious Lord" by our choirs. A young Elvis sang several early hits. Everything was designed to lead toward the appearance of Elvis himself. Periodically, someone would announce his whereabouts: "Elvis has left the hotel. Elvis is in the limousine!" You could feel the anticipation! In addition, HBN-TV (Heavenly Broadcast Network) sponsored "Elvis in Concert" and videotaped the service. As part of the arrangement, Elvis agreed to a live interview.

Our children's story was based on, "Don't Be Cruel." Sometimes we are cruel: Brothers hit sisters. Sisters slap brothers. We tell lies about our friends. But God didn't mean for us to be cruel. The Bible says, "Always be full of joy in the Lord. I say it again – rejoice! Let everyone see that you are considerate in all you do." (Philippians 4:4-5) So, "**Don't be Cruel**" to your friends or to your "**Hound Dog**" because you might get "**All Shook Up**," break our "**Wooden Hearts**" and send us "**Crying in the Chapel**" or to the "**Heartbreak Hotel**" where we'd be singing "**Jailhouse Rock**." Instead, follow Jesus, read the Bible and "**Love Me Tender**" then you can "**Let me be your Teddy Bear**." When it comes to being nice: "**It's Now or Never**" before someone gets mad and says to you, "**Return to Sender**." (Corny but fun!)

As the kids went back to their seats, the announcer's voice boomed: "The limousine has just pulled in!" "Elvis Presley has entered the building!" It's been years but Elvis is back. What would he say? Or sing? More importantly, what does Elvis have to do with me and my relationship with God? Maybe I should let Elvis answer for himself. With 2001 Space Odyssey in the background, the announcer proclaimed: "He's been gone for many years but now he's back! The king of rock and roll, the one and only… Elvis!"

As the crowd screamed, Elvis, accompanied by three bodyguards ran down the center aisle. His suit was black with a full cape and loaded with sequins. He looked like Elvis, but would he sing like Elvis? The first song was "That's Alright Mamma" then Elvis began the song that convinced us all: "Wise men say only fools rush in but I can't help falling in love with you." As the applause died down, a voice came over the loudspeaker: "Elvis, I'm with the HBN Heavenly Broadcast Network and I would like to ask you a few questions. Of course, all of us would like to know… Where have you been?"

Next: The Interview continues. Who is that voice interviewing Elvis?

August 27 - Elvis & The Interview

Matthew 5:17-48

"Elvis, I'm with the HBN Heavenly Broadcast Network and I would like to ask you a few questions. Of course, all of us would like to know… Where have you been?"

Elvis replied: "Well, for the last month I've been on a diet so I could fit in this suit. I've been eating a few too many fried peanut butter and banana sandwiches. As far as what I've been doing: For a while, I hung out at Graceland."

The voice continued: "What about your beginnings? How did you get started singing and what were the early years like?"

"They, say when I was 3 years old," Elvis continued. "I got away from my parents in church and walked in front of the choir and started beating time on my leg. I loved gospel music. I wanted to be a gospel singer, but they told me I couldn't harmonize. Can you believe that? Gospel music will always hold a special place in my heart."

"Elvis, you served in the military when you didn't have to. Why?"

"I'm very proud of my time in the Army. I love my country and felt the right way to serve was to do what everyone else had to do. They wanted me to go into Special Services and sing but I just wanted to be another soldier. I was a sergeant when I got out. I'm proud to say this will always be one of my greatest achievements. Of course, the best thing that happened was I met my future wife, Priscilla."

"Is this when you became a drug addict?" the interviewer asked. Elvis.

Presley's face burned in obvious irritation. The interview was not going as expected. Regaining his composure, Elvis replied: "I was never a drug addict. President Nixon awarded me a badge to serve our country. Yes, I take sleeping pills, you can't imagine what it's like after a concert. During the day I take Dexedrine to wake up and get going again. But everything is prescribed by my doctor."

There was a moment of silence before the interviewer continued: "Elvis, you still sing a lot of Gospel, but your faith and your lifestyle do not reflect the music you claim to love. You are hopelessly addicted to prescription drugs!"

"Who are you and just who do you think you're talking to!" Elvis screamed and at the same time gestured to a bodyguard, "Find that Heavenly Broadcast idiot and bring him here." Long agonizingly silent minutes pass before the bodyguard appeared and shrugged. Elvis was stunned: "Well, where is he?" He looked around frantically. "Where are you?"

Next: The Mystery Voice Revealed

August 28 - Elvis: The Mystery Voice Revealed

Matthew 5:1-12

The interview did not go well. The bodyguard looked everywhere but couldn't find the mystery voice. Elvis looked around frantically. "Where are you? Who are you?"

"I'm still here, Elvis. Who do you think I am?"

"Where is here? Who is here?" Suddenly, Elvis realizes the obvious answer. "Are you trying to tell me that you are God?"

"Yes, and I'm disappointed, Elvis. You could have influenced millions to follow me through your gift of music. Instead, you did everything to suit yourself."

There was a long pause as the King of Rock and Roll gathered his thoughts. Slowly Elvis began to talk: "God, I've always known there had to be a greater purpose for me. I read the Bible and sang gospel music with passion. I guess the true meaning was right in front of me. I missed a great opportunity to serve. If only I could live my life over again. Can you ever forgive me?"

God replied, "Elvis, I've already forgiven you. You are a wonderful person, blessed with many unique talents but I put you on this earth to use those God given talents wisely. What's important is what will you do now?"

Elvis said, "Lord, I always loved, 'You'll Never Walk Alone' but I haven't sung it in a while. The words are simple and short, but the meaning seems appropriate now. I know that faith is truly one of the greatest gifts offered by You. With faith I know that I'll never have to walk alone again. Thank you, Lord!"

There was a pause before God spoke: "Elvis, sing so the others will see me through your talents." With passion born anew by restored faith in almighty God, Elvis sang as only he can:

> When you walk through a storm,
> hold your head up high and don't be afraid of the dark.
> At the end of the storm is a golden sky and the sweet silver song of a lark.
> Walk on through the wind.
> Walk on through the rain though your dreams be tossed and blown.
> Walk on. Walk on with hope in your heart and you'll never walk alone.
> You'll never walk alone.

Prayer Challenge: Lord, I go my own way often. Thank you for Your amazing grace!

August 29 - Hope

Psalm 9

It's been a long hard week. The Stock Market reports look more like a roller coaster ride. Our economy acts much like the kid sitting in the first seat of the coaster looking nauseous. Violence and unrest in the Mid East continue. The news features more stories of lay-offs, accounting scandals and corporate bankruptcies. I could loudly complain or bury my head in the sand. I could stay up all night and worry myself sick. But, as a minister, I learned that often during strife God displays a miracle of hope.

For two years, a church member faithfully cared for her mother after she was diagnosed with cancer and a form of dementia. At first, it was difficult but there were bright moments. Our church organized a "Bridge" club so she could enjoy her favorite pastime. Her moments of forgetfulness and mood swings were endured as a phase of her disease. Then, her mother's condition slowly worsened. Even the "Bridge" outings had to be cancelled. As the cancer spread, the dementia took its toll on everyone as her mother became increasingly frustrated, suspicious, and moody. Often in this situation, the mother becomes a child: rebellious and argumentative. Yet, throughout the whole ordeal, her daughter continued to lovingly care for her. It wasn't easy. Occasionally, she would retreat to the church to pray, to think and to cry.

Then, her mother had a stroke and was admitted to the hospital. By this time, she no longer recognized anyone, and her occasional conversations could more accurately be described as incoherent ramblings. But she was also waving her arms more and at times even looked like she was holding an imaginary pen and attempting to write something. Honestly, no one thought anything of it. An alert nurse noticed the gestures and suggested that she put a pen in her mother's hand and place a sheet of paper underneath. "I thought it was silly," she told me later but reluctantly followed the nurse's instructions. Her mother paused for a moment and then she began to slowly and deliberately write: "I love you." Four days later, she passed away.

In one special moment, the daughter's two-year long struggle was made worthwhile. She and her family will always treasure that single piece of paper. What about you? Do you need a miracle of hope within your roller coaster ride of life? Look at the promises from God: "For the needy will not be forgotten forever; the hopes of the poor will not always be crushed." (Psalm 9:18) "In sudden fear I cried, I have been cut off from the Lord! But you heard my cry for mercy and answered my call for help. So be strong and take courage, all you who put your hope in the Lord!"

Two promises: 1. You will not be forgotten. 2. Be strong and take courage. The stock market is still a roller coaster ride. The Mid-East situation is volatile. But God is firmly in charge. I will never be forgotten. God gives me strength and provides hope. I know a daughter who will say a loud, "Amen!" to that.

Prayer Challenge: Lord, help me find hope during my struggles.

August 30 - Monkeys

Matthew 7:24-29

My mother-in-law sent me an article from her hometown newspaper titled: Monkeys pelt cars with fruit. "Three monkeys pelted cars on Interstate 95 with bananas and crab apples before running across the highway and fleeing into the woods. A woman flagged down a state trooper and told him a monkey had thrown an apple at her car. At that moment a crab apple came out of nearby trees and hit the van. 'Lo and behold there were three brown monkeys in a tree throwing crab apples.'"

Life can be full of surprises. You're cruising the highway minding your own business when suddenly: SPLAT! A monkey throws a crab apple, smashing your windshield, squashing your routine and your day. There is a phone call from the doctor who wants to see you or the Internal Revenue Service letter saying: audit. An interoffice memo announces your company plans to downsize. Your child brings home a note from school: "Come to the principal's office!" A message from your spouse: "We need to talk!"

Squash! Abruptly, your peaceful journey is shattered. All resources must now be focused on this latest crisis. Do you resume your trip and pretend nothing happened? Do you stop to investigate? Do you wait and hope the crisis will go away? Should you call for help? Instead of being in control, you become a helpless target worrying over what the monkeys might throw next.

Jesus told a story about two builders. The foolish one built a house on a foundation of sand. The inevitable storms arrived, the rain came down, the winds blew and beat against the house, and it collapsed. The wise builder used a foundation of rock. "The rain came down, the streams rose, the winds blew and beat against the house; yet it did not fall." (Mat. 7:25) Both builders faced the same storms but only one house survived. The secret to survival lies within the foundation.

When storm winds blow, and fruit starts flying it's wise to remember: Reverence for the Lord is the foundation of true wisdom. (Psalm 111:10) God's truth stands firm like a foundation stone. (2 Timothy 2:19) After you have suffered a little while, he will restore, support, and strengthen you and place you on a firm foundation. (1 Peter 5:10) You, dear friends, must continue to build your lives on the foundation of your holy faith. And continue to pray as you are directed by the Holy Spirit. (Jude 1:20)

Are you feeling the sting of a monkey's crab apple attack? Has your journey been sidetracked by crisis? Maybe this is a good time to build on the foundation of your faith. Does your relationship with God need a little strengthening? When is the last time you attended a Bible study? Prayed with someone? Talked with your pastor? It's never too late, you know. And another thing, watch out for flying fruit.

Prayer Challenge: What can you do to strengthen your foundation?

August 31 - A Cure for Identity Crisis

Psalm 139

"O Lord, you examined my heart and know everything about me. You know when I sit down or stand up. You know my every thought when far away." (139:1-2)

Do you ever feel insignificant? Others run faster, jump farther. Another is more successful. No matter how talented and gifted you may be, there is someone who is better, faster, or more creative. Modern science doesn't help. The universe is expanding while our planet in comparison seems just an inconsequential speck. Computers do our work and do it faster and more efficiently. It's easy to look around and feel insignificant. Are you having an identity crisis? You are not alone, but God has a cure: Psalm 139.

Would it surprise you to find that the author of Psalm 139 was having his own identity crisis? David, the slayer of giants, gifted poet and powerful king doubted himself? It's true and those doubts make Psalm 139 one of his best. David is asking and answering important questions about his struggle for self-identity.

Does God really know me? "You chart the path ahead of me and tell me where to stop and rest.

Every moment you know where I am." (v3) This is an involved God who cares about every moment of your life. Matthew 10:30 adds, "the very hairs of your head are numbered." God really does know you: Intimately!

Does God seem far away? "I can never escape from your spirit! If I go up to heaven, you are there; if I go down to the place of the dead, you are there." (v7) The promise is clear that wherever you go, God is there. Are you feeling abandoned? God is close to you: Close enough to really care!

Are you feeling worthless? "You made all the delicate, inner parts of my body and knit me together in my mother's womb. Thank you for making me so wonderfully complex! Your workmanship is marvelous." (v13) God is carefully working within your mother's womb to create the miracle soon to be born… you.

Will God really protect me from evil? I am so afraid! At first, David expresses righteous indignation towards those who hate God. But then, David realizes evil is not just in others but is also deeply rooted within. David concludes: "Search me, O God and know my heart; test me and know my anxious thoughts. See if there is any offensive way in me and lead me in the way everlasting." (23-24) Instead of looking to God to protect him from others, David looks inward. God protects you: From without and from within!

Are you having an identity crisis? God knows you intimately and promises to remain close. God carefully made you and will protect you by removing the evil from within. The proof is in the Psalmist's life as God transforms a shepherd boy into a mighty king.

Prayer Challenge: Read Psalm 139 and see how much God loves you.

September

September 1 - Katrina And Twenty Beds

1 Peter 4:8-11

Hurricane Katrina roared through southern Mississippi and Louisiana. For days, an anxious world watched the plight of thousands trapped in the New Orleans Astrodome and wondered: "When would help finally arrive? Yet, for every horrible story, there were more acts of compassion and heroism: The dramatic helicopter rescue of thousands stranded on rooftops. Neighbors who banded together to help each other and those in need. A nurse tearfully admitting losing everything while at the hospital helping others.

Around the country ordinary people responded with generosity and compassion. Our church received enough supplies to completely fill up a large tractor trailer. Literally thousands of people brought supplies and donations. Many were going to multiple locations looking for any opportunity to contribute to the relief effort. One family, newly arrived from New Orleans drove up and asked if we were collecting for the hurricane. They saw what we were doing and wanted to thank us. The pastor of a church in Gulfport, Mississippi invited our church to send a team and deliver supplies. Plus, we had two police cars to deliver, donated by our sheriff's department.

One person suggested we purchase beds to replace the thousands ruined in the flooding. I received a special price on twenty mattress and bed sets while employees of the same store purchased sheets. While driving to Mississippi, I questioned the wisdom of spending so much money on beds and wondered if they would be used.

The Apostle Peter wrote: "God has given gifts to each of you from his great variety of spiritual gifts. Manage them well so that God's generosity can flow through you. (1 Peter 4:10) For me, this meant using my gifts and those of our team to trust God and do God's work. If we are willing to take the risk and make the journey, God would do the rest. We drove all night and arrived early the next morning at a distribution site where we sought places to deliver the materials. We knew God was guiding our mission when the pastor who invited us asked if we could procure beds for the relief workers. Almost choking with emotion, I asked: "How many do you need?"

"I'm not sure," the pastor replied. "Maybe twenty?" My exhaustion vanished as I shared the story with the group. Later that same afternoon we visited the church and helped unload those beds. The kitchen and halls of the church were converted to storage and feeding areas. Sunday school classes became bedrooms. In the sanctuary, pews were moved for the relief workers and our twenty beds. The Pastor said, "More than forty percent of our congregation lost their homes. Many more lost their jobs." But he also talked about helping thousands of people receive supplies and comfort.

At the front entrance of the church, we met a lady greeting those in line needing aid and helping them fill out paperwork. She considered herself a missionary of comfort greeting each person with a tender, "Hi sweetie! May I give you a hug? While you're filling out the forms, please tell me what happened and how you're doing?" She would listen to each story carefully with tender compassion. She personally escorted them to receive aid and then cheerfully walked with them back to their car.

In just one day, we saw God's miraculous hand at work bringing beds exactly where they were needed, showing us a church on the front lines helping others despite their own severe losses and we witnessed the tender witness of a woman who offered God's extraordinary encouragement and love.

Next: Catastrophe and Hope

September 2 - Catastrophe, Hope & A Lighthouse

James chapter 2

The next day, after arriving in Gulfport, Mississippi, we drove to the waterfront area to witness the damage from Hurricane Katrina firsthand. No words can describe the enormity of the destruction for miles all around us. The few trees which were still standing were strewn with paper and plastic over twenty feet high. Looking up, you had to wonder how trash could possibly end up so high in the air. Then you realized we were looking at the water level. How could it possibly be? Realizing the enormity of so much water sent cold chills through us all.

In place of buildings, you often saw piles of debris near cement foundations. Automobiles were buried in the sand or stacked on top of each other. Virtually everything was destroyed. Yet in the front yard of one house was an ominous sign: "You loot, we shoot." The owner stood guard with his gun cocked. We also witnessed many signs of hope amidst the ruins. Several people drove by to offer food and other assistance. One man unloaded several boxes of canned food and bottled water. He said simply: "I have more than I need and just want to share."

"Dear brothers and sisters, what's the use of saying you have faith if you don't prove it by your actions?

That kind of faith can't save anyone. Suppose you see a brother or sister who needs food or clothing, and you say, "Well, good-bye and God bless you; stay warm and eat well"—but then you don't give that person any food or clothing. What good does that do?" (James 2:14-16)

All the sermons in the world will never adequately show our love to the people affected by the hurricane. Our actions speak so much louder than mere words. What we saw in Mississippi was devastation beyond our imagination, yet we also witnessed miracles and so many poignant gestures of Gods amazing love.

That evening, while everyone slept, I printed photographs of the damage. One picture featured a lighthouse, the only building still standing on that stretch of beach. Piled all around the lighthouse was debris from the storm. That lighthouse in many ways represented our mission: A light still standing amidst the storm. Our team wanted to be a lighthouse for the people affected by Katrina. That lighthouse standing strong against the storm reinforced and revitalized our own mission of hope.

All too soon, it was time to leave Mississippi for the trip home. While saying good-bye to our hosts and newfound friends, we began a new mission which kept us working together for years.

Prayer Challenge: How can God guide you to be a lighthouse for others?

September 3 - After Katrina

Luke 3:18-21

Four years after Hurricane Katrina ravaged the Gulf Coast, I travelled back to Gulfport, Mississippi with a church group building a new house. I had the opportunity to see how much the area was rebuilt since Katrina. At first glance there were visible signs of prosperity. Glitzy casinos advertised the latest payout and featured entertainers. There were shopping malls, gift shops and restaurants everywhere. But there was something else – something different, that you couldn't help but notice.

Beside the new restaurant was an abandoned lot. In between a casino and a novelty shop were empty properties displaying a concrete foundation, surrounded by weeds. Everywhere you travelled you saw signs of normalcy beside images of tragedy. The stamp of Katrina was still prevalent. Beach front property once occupied by stately old mansions now contained a few new houses beside government issues trailers and abandoned lots. "There is no middle ground," said the pastor of a nearby church. "Everywhere you turn there are signs of prosperity and signs of poverty. Most of us would still be in trailers, if not for the work of churches all over the country."

He should know. For the past four years, his church served as host to thousands of church volunteers who came from all over the country to either repair existing homes or build new ones. The upstairs education building was converted to sleep volunteers. A bunk house with showers, kitchen and a gathering room was built behind the church. Supplies are stored in two warehouses nearby. All in all, nearly 100 volunteers continually live, and work and they are all supplied at this one church.

Our work group was made up of preachers, retired professionals and a few who took a vacation from active careers. Each day our group along with three other groups shared food and cooking duties. We were helping to build a new house for a woman who was disabled and her father. We each were assigned jobs to match our experience. Carpenters were soon installing crown molding and building a deck while those of us less experienced were installing flooring or painting. Local residents often joined us providing snacks, expressing appreciation, and telling stories about their experiences during Hurricane Katrina.

Each night, we returned to the church to clean up, eat dinner, gather for devotions, and share our experiences. During one session, a retired University Professor stood and shared his struggles with finding a meaningful relationship with God. "God seems to talk to others," he said. "Why won't he talk to me?" Shortly after retirement his wife unexpectedly died of cancer. Devastated by the loss, the professor described his struggle with grief but also spoke of the many friends who surrounded him with love.

Frustrated, with his constant nagging, Jim finally asked: "What do you want me to do?" One friend suggested he start a Bible study. "A Bible Study? Why would I do that?" He himself did not understand what prompted him to say, "Yes." Yet, it was that men's Bible study that helped him discover God had been talking to him all along. While helping others understand the Bible, the professor deepened his own relationship with God. Clear proof of God's handiwork was evidenced by the men surrounding him that night who were in Mississippi because of his Bible study. Later, one of our men commented: "It was worth coming to Mississippi just to hear the professor."

Jesus said, "What is the Kingdom of God like? How can I illustrate it? It is like a tiny mustard seed that a man planted in a garden; it grows and becomes a tree, and the birds make nests in its branches." He also asked, "What else is the Kingdom of God like? It is like the yeast a woman used in making bread. Even though she put only a little yeast in three measures of flour, it permeated every part of the dough."
(Luke 13:18-21)

I like to think that our mission trip, like thousands of others, was part of a tiny mustard seed that grows and becomes a tree or yeast that permeates every part of the dough. In our own way, we made a difference for someone, for a community and for ourselves.

Prayer Challenge: How has God touched your life through helping others?

September 4 - What's Wrong with my Parrot?

Psalm 119:97-112

Chuck Swindol wrote about a lady who went to the pet store to buy a parrot. She was assured she would have a friend for years. A week later she returned to complain that her bird was not talking. "Did you buy a mirror?" asked the owner. "When parrots look at themselves, words flow." She bought a mirror.

A few days later, she complained that her bird still hadn't uttered a peep. "Did you get a ladder? Parrots love to climb and need to feel comfortable." She bought a ladder. Later, she returned grim and disappointed: No parrot talk. "Have you bought a swing?" She attached a swing. Three days later she stormed in and demanded to speak to the owner. "He died this afternoon!" she blurted out.

"Died! Did he ever talk?" asked the owner. "Yes," she responded. "He said just a few words as he breathed his last. 'Don't they sell any food at that store?'"

Swindol added, "We live in a day of religious mirrors, ladders, and swings where the majority of hungry souls are given empty promises and sold a bill of goods. There are lots of trinkets and gimmicks but no food."

It's like the commercial featuring a sweet little old lady standing at a fast-food counter holding two buns and asking: "Where's the beef?" It may be time to ask of your own spiritual life: "Where's the beef?"

The Bible says: "How sweet are your words to my taste; they are sweeter than honey. Your commandments give me understanding; no wonder I hate every false way of life. Your word is a lamp for my feet and a light for my path." (Psalm 119: 103-105) Look at the promises: How sweet are your words. Your commandments give me understanding. Your Word is a lamp and a light.

At a Bible study graduation for a group of high school students, you could feel their excitement as they shared their stories. Over the past nine months these young people met every Wednesday evening and together, they studied nearly eighty per cent of the Bible. Seeing their enthusiasm and energy inspired me to renew my own commitment as a pastor and writer. What about you?

Have you fed the 'parrot' lately? What are you doing to strengthen your spiritual life? When is the last time you participated in a good Bible study? "Where is the beef?" Is your spiritual life challenging? Does your church strive to teach God's Word? How can you help? Do you have a disciplined prayer life? Are you sharing your food? Are you involved with a local church? Do you serve a ministry that is reaching out to the community? If someone had a problem, would they come to you?

Somewhere, there is a heavenly "store" waiting to serve you. You will find a few mirrors, maybe a ladder or a swing but you don't notice those right away. What you immediately discover is the main aisle. Like a magnet, you are drawn to the mouth-watering variety of delicious spiritual food, lots of food.

Prayer Challenge: What can you do today to feed your "parrot?"

September 5 - Windshield or Bug?

Matthew 7:24-29

One quiet Monday morning, I received an ominous phone call: "Rev. Davies, this is the high school. Your son is not in school today."

"You must be mistaken," I said, trying to sound calm. "He left the house on time. Are you sure, he's not there?"

"Yes sir. Our policy is to notify parents when students are absent or tardy. Our records show your son as absent," replied the calm professional voice.

As my heart pounded my voice remained calm: "Thanks for letting me know."

Like any parent with a sixteen-year-old son, I panicked! My car nearly did a wheelie out of the driveway as I flew down the road toward the high school. "Has he been in an accident?" I thought. "Oh God, please protect my son. Maybe he's skipping school with friends." I wondered. "I'll kill him! I'll take his car keys away and he'll ride the bus! He'll be grounded for a month! A year! For LIFE!!!"

While screeching into the parking lot, I noticed a car that could only be my child's. After running into the office and checking with the secretary, I was assured my son was safe inside the classroom. "Whew! I can breathe again!"

Have you heard the country song: "Sometimes you're the windshield; sometimes the bug?" I'm beginning to understand what that means. In the few short seconds of one phone call, the peace and tranquility of my "windshield" morning was shattered. Instead of being in control, I was a helpless "bug" hurtling down the highway with no way of knowing what tragedy would occur next.

This time, nothing happened but what about next time? I always try to remain a "windshield," but I know there will be those "bug" moments. I may even get squashed!

Jesus told a story of two builders. The foolish one built a house on a foundation of sand. When the inevitable storm came, the house collapsed. However, the wise builder built a house on a foundation of rock so when the inevitable storms came the house stood strong. Both builders faced the same storms. The secret was in the foundation.

God never promised a storm-free, bug-free life. However, Jesus does promise to provide a solid foundation to weather the rain and the wind and shield you during those occasional "bug" moments. Windshield or bug kind of day? Storms? Those, you seldom control. Rock or sand? Choose wisely and you will have the solid foundation you need.

Prayer Challenge: How can you strengthen your foundation?

September 6 - Where Are You God?

2 Corinthians chapter 4

It's been an emotionally draining month. The kind that makes you want cry out: "Where are you God?" A beautiful 19-month-old boy is dying of cancer. A young couple is about to separate. Three different people lost a loved one. Another young man is in jail struggling with a drug problem. A woman continues her battle against cancer. Another woman is desperately trying to break the pervasive hold of an abusive relationship.

Where is God during a tragedy? Where is the hope? Paul, sick and in prison, was writing to a church also experiencing hardships. Yet surrounded by hopelessness, Paul speaks of hope: "We are pressed on every side by troubles, but we are not crushed and broken. We are perplexed, but we don't give up and quit. We are hunted down, but God never abandons us. We get knocked down, but we get up again." (2 Corinthians 4:8-9)

How does Paul maintain his faith? He writes: "That is why we never give up. Though our bodies are dying, our spirits are renewed every day. For our present troubles are quite small and won't last very long. Yet they produce for us an immeasurably great glory that will last forever! So, we don't look at the troubles we see right now; rather, we look forward to what we have not yet seen. For the troubles we see will soon be over, but the joys to come will last forever." (2 Cor 4:16-18)

Your body may be dying but with trust and faith, your spirit will strengthen. The suffering you experience now will be replaced with God's glory which lasts an eternity. We learn to look beyond our troubles to the joys of God's promises!

How do we do that? God formed the church. Although filled with imperfect human beings, the church is still the best place I know to receive comfort and hope. During this same month: The family of the dying baby received love and support from around the community. A man struggling with career problems found a new job with great potential. Several women in a Bible study described times when the love shared by the group helped them cope with unspeakable pain. The woman breaking free from an abusive relationship is now seeing someone who genuinely cares about her. Together they are working toward a deeper faith. A visitor shares how God changed his life.

Where is God? Paul answered: "For the troubles we see will soon be over, but the joys to come will last forever." If you are looking for God, don't give up, pray, reach out to a friend, look to your church, open your Bible and God will find you!

Prayer Challenge: Are you experiencing troubles? Read 2 Corinthians 4.

September 7 - Readers Give Thanks

James 5:13-18

"I've been reading your devotions for years. At first, I was in total despair. I left my husband because of his abuse. My oldest daughter was an addict. I didn't have a job and couldn't support my two children. I was lonely and did not know if I had the will to go on. But some of the people with your ministry who emailed me became friends and I have prayed for others and hope I have been able to help them through their struggles."

Sowing Seeds Ministry sends out encouraging devotions every week. Also, each week, we receive letters that tell stories of lives touched by God. Here are a few of them.

"I don't know where to begin to tell you how blessed my family and I have been. Let me tell you some of the major prayers that have been answered for me this year. I have two friends from my church that have survived cancer, our business is booming, my daughter is doing great in college and my husband's nephew is surviving deployment overseas. Thank you for your ministry and God bless you."

A Daily Dose of Godly Encouragement: Medicine for Tough Days

"I enjoy receiving your devotions. I copy a lot of them and read them to my Sunday School Class. We range in age from 80 to 90 and it is always a blessing to read something like this to them."

"Your devotions have done much to educate me in the ways of Christ. They showed me how blessed I am even in the worst circumstances because there are so many hurting souls. Praying for them makes my troubles disappear and I am thankful."

"When everything seemed to go wrong, I felt God's warm grace. I was nearly lost to despair when I wrote and was astounded to find people prayed for me. I am sure the prayers made the difference as I was starting to feel better after months of severe depression. I will be attending church services tomorrow for the first time in months. I am ready to hear the word of the Lord again. I felt so unworthy. Thank you."

"Although I'm losing my home and have nowhere for my family to go, the prayers and emails I received saved my life. I was contemplating suicide. I'm not going to tell you that I don't think about it still but it's not an option. Since I started reading these devotions I have gone back to church. I can't thank you enough."

"I heard from people all over the world. I developed a friendship with a girl from India. Each week I read the prayer requests and write a word of encouragement. I also forward prayer requests to those women in our group. You will probably never know how your ministry has touched so many lives."

Prayer Challenge: Who can you pray for today? How can you be part of the answer?

September 8 – "Do It Again"

Psalm 145

Drayton Hawthorne described tense moments while waiting for his wife Robin's surgery. He said: "She was outside looking at the stars. I thought it was settled and done. Her surgery was a few days away and although the doctors assured her this was a routine procedure, she was still looking as if they were going to amputate something!"

"As her husband, I assumed my duty was to hide concern while showing a strong front. Like most men, I substituted statistics and reason for assurance and thought it was enough. Now she was worrying again. I walked toward her ready to offer more of my male logic. But that's when the miracle happened. Everything I planned to say vanished. Unknown words came from my lips, as I silently wrapped my arms around her waist and kissed her cheek. 'God loves you. Everything will be all right. You will see a shooting star as my promise that you will be ok.'"

"In an instant the most spectacular shooting star we ever saw blazed across the sky from horizon to horizon. A surprised and delighted, "Ooh!" came from my wife! For a long moment neither of us spoke. What could we say? Moments before, I was an insensitive, scolding husband walking towards a fearful, anxious wife.

Somehow, God miraculously intervened and changed us both into vessels of His gracious love."

Usually, our influence is a steady, consistent attitude of faith. People know and remember us by our day-to-day actions among our family and friends. Occasionally, there are life-changing moments when God's influence suddenly shines and the only word that adequately describes what happens next is miracle.

Drayton continued: "Being an instrument of God's will, at times may not be voluntary or even expected. I always believed God would use me only if I asked and was spiritually clean. Sometimes, this is true but not in my case. God interrupted my mission and substituted His own. I wanted to comfort Robin with common sense and almost interrupted a miraculous moment of faith. No matter the reason for why it happens, when God, uses you for whatever purpose, you will feel blessed because of it."

"Thinking of the wonderful moment we shared with God is very emotional for me. Several times in telling our shooting star story my wife would need to finish because I became too 'choked up' so once more I will let her finish…"

Robin smiled and then said: "After we stood there a few moments just soaking in what happened, I turned to my husband and whispered, 'Do it again!'"

Prayer Challenge: Who needs to hear this amazing story? Share it with them.

September 9 - Pianos, Rats and Born Again

John chapter 3

Musicians at a nightclub were complaining about an old piano. The keys would stick, and the sound was hideous. After months of listening to the grumbling and whining the owner finally decided to do something about it. He had the piano painted. Painted? What good would that do? In our walk with God, do we settle for a paint job when we really need a tune up? It's easy to play Christian without acting like one. We seek comfort, instead of a challenge. You want rest, not responsibility. I all too readily accept peace, and surrender passion. We look for a paint brush rather than a toolbox.

Nicodemus had been painting his piano for years before meeting Jesus. A high-ranking religious leader, Nicodemus could be the preacher of your church, but something was missing. Jesus looked deep into Nicodemus' heart and said: "I assure you unless you are born again you can never see the kingdom of God." (John 3:3) Nicodemus was confused: "I thought being "born again" was for others, not me! I don't want to change, too much." A minister wrote, "I love Jesus, but I want to hold on to my own friends, to my own independence, to the respect of my professional colleagues, to my own plans."

We would rather paint our piano, but Jesus says, "For God so loved the world that he gave his only Son, so that everyone who believes in Him will not perish but have eternal life." (John 3:16) God paid the ultimate price so that we inherit a promise and a purpose. The promise? "God will never abandon you." Our purpose? Offer that same astonishing promise to others. But, when it comes to offering the promise of God to others, we have a lot to learn.

Sue Bates a missionary in Romania wrote about a worker who takes clothing and medicine to the streets every few months but doesn't get too involved. He was talking to a 12-year-old boy about Jesus, but he was getting nowhere. So, he asked the boy, "Why can't you believe in a God of love?"

The boy thought for a second and then asked, "Why do rats scream at night?" The worker complained: "See, I tried to talk about God, but it was like talking to a wall. He wasn't listening, and then he talked about rats. Those kids are hopeless."

Maybe, it was the missionary who wasn't listening. He drove a nice car, wore nice clothes, slept in a comfortable bed, had a family and plenty of money to spend. The street kid had almost nothing: a filthy "bed" in a stinking hole underground that had roaches, lice, fleas, and rats that screamed at night. The boy's message was plain and to the point. "You asked why I can't believe in a God of love? Tell me why rats scream at night. Then maybe you can figure why I struggle to believe."

Jesus came into our dark world and became "one of us." Are we willing to learn by Christ's example? Perhaps, too often we want the best of both worlds. How can we have compassion for others, if we refuse to allow God to "tune our piano" and help us become "born again?" Is your piano sounding a bit out of tune: A little beat up inside? You could simply repaint it? Or you could expose yourself to the penetrating and healing light of Christ. Sue Bates ends her story, "I didn't know rats screamed at night. Did you?" Perhaps my piano needs a tune up too.

Prayer Challenge: God, I too quickly settle for a coat of paint instead of a tune up.

September 10 - Coping with Grief: Joel Warren

2 Corinthians 1:3-7

"I hurt so much and want so badly to have Marlyn back. I never thought I could miss someone so much. I told her once that I couldn't really sleep unless I was "plugged in" to her." Joel Warren wrote this shortly after his wife, Marlyn died of cancer. For therapy, he began to write about his feelings and experiences. The following poem is one of many he wrote while learning to cope.

The light in my life has gone out. The candle to my soul no longer burns.
All that remains is a dark hole.

My limbs still move through, day to day tasks.
While in my heart: why, why, I ask?

The answer I may never know, why I should stay and she must go.
I long for her voice, the touch of her hand --
Why please God, help me to understand.

My chores here on earth are not through, but someday, I'll return to you.

But between this day and who knows when –
You'll always be my wife and friend. My wife, my life,
my Marlyn.

There are no magic words of comfort to ease the pain of grief. Joel describes his loss as a light going out with nothing remaining but a "deep dark hole." The first stage of grief is often called the "Survival stage." Joel describes it as, "My limbs still move through day-to-day tasks" as if they are not really a part of his body.

Another part of grief is called a "Questioning stage." This is when you ask: Why? Why did this have to happen? Why did God let it happen? Joel writes, "Why, why, I ask? The answer I may never know, why I should stay, and she must go."

A third phase of grief is the "Coping stage." It does not mean you necessarily understand the answer to the why questions. Coping is better described as accepting the lack of a good answer to "why." Joel writes, "My chores here on earth are not through, but someday I'll return to you."

Joel wrote: "I've started to rearrange things in the house. As I move furniture or other items from the places my wife chose, in my heart I feel another door close. I'm not shutting out these memories but storing them in a special part of me. It remains a room in my heart, and it will always be a special part of who I am." Joel Warren found a way to express the pain of loss and helped himself and others cope. "The future looks much brighter now as I look forward to when and how!"

Prayer Challenge: How can you or your church help someone who is grieving?

September 11 - Ground Zero

2 Corinthians chapter 4

The 9/11 Memorial is no ordinary tourist attraction. We were enjoying the sights and sounds of New York City but once we stepped on "Ground Zero" the laughter and chatter ceased. We were fellow mourners paying our respects. The 9/11 attacks killed 2,977 people from more than 90 countries. Most of us remember where we were on that tragic day. I could not visit New York without paying my respects.

The 9/11 Memorial opened ten years after the attacks. There are two pools set in the foundation of the former twin towers. Thirty-foot waterfalls - described in the brochure as the largest in North America - pour into the pools and then vanish in the center. The names of every victim are inscribed in bronze around the pools. As I leaned over the wall to gaze at the waterfall, I couldn't help but rub my hand over the engraved names and pronounce each one out loud. Some of the names were familiar. Like many churches, ours regularly listed the names and we prayed for their families.

Surrounding the pools are Swamp White Oak trees planted to add peace and serenity. One solitary pear tree is the "Survivor Tree." Badly damaged, near death, the tree was discovered shortly after the tragedy and nursed back to health. The "Survivor Tree" is now over 30 feet tall and stands as a testimony to the fortitude of the survivors.

Also on site is the museum which has become the central location for preserving the history of the tragedy. Located in the space between the North and South Towers, the museum is designed to help you relive what happened that day but also chronicles the stories of the survivors as they and the city rebuild. As you walk through the halls, you hear stories about the victims, view dozens of media images and even touch objects found near the site. There is the Ladder Company 3 Fire Truck smashed by chunks of debris. There is the Giant Cross made of two steel beams that stood at "Ground Zero." One hall is called "102 Minutes: Events of the Day" helping you relive what happened during the 102 minutes between the impact of the first plane into the North Tower to the crash of the fourth plane in Pennsylvania.

One exhibit displayed a motorcycle named the "Dream Bike." According to the description: "Firefighter Gerard Baptiste purchased a battered Honda motorcycle in order to restore it to good working order. Following Baptiste's death on 9/11, surviving members of the firehouse and motorcycle enthusiasts nationwide, transformed the motorcycle into a "bike of healing' known as the Dream Bike. Ten roses painted on the cover of its gas tank symbolize the members of Engine Company 33 killed that day."

Near the end of your museum tour, you are invited to watch a multi-screen 360 surround film experience appropriately named "Rebirth at Ground Zero" which uses time lapse footage and interviews to show the rebuilding and renewal of the World Trade Center site. Upon leaving the museum you can't help but notice the newly built World Trade Center towering above the memorial and the museum grounds.

I came to pay my respects, but I left the 9/11 Memorial and Museum with a sense of awe and pride at the resilience and fortitude of the survivors. 9/11 will always be a tragic day burned into our memory, but that day may ultimately be one of America's greatest examples of triumph in the face of tragedy, accomplishment in the midst of destruction.

Paul wrote in a letter to the Corinthians, "We are hard pressed on every side but not crushed; perplexed but not in despair; persecuted but not abandoned; struck down but not destroyed." (2 Cor 4:8) Could this be the ultimate lesson of 9/11? No matter what you may be going through? We are hard pressed on every side but not crushed. Whatever problems you may be facing? We are perplexed but not in despair. No matter who you may be dealing with! We are persecuted but not abandoned. Whatever tragedy you may be facing! We are struck down but not destroyed.

The gospel of John says: "I give them eternal life and they shall never perish; no one can snatch them out of my hands." (10:28)

Prayer Challenge: How can we share and learn from the 9/11 tragedy?

September 12 - A Professor the Mideast & Depression

1 John 1:1-5

"Visiting Israel changed my life but not in the way you think," a retiring professor said at a ceremony honoring his years of service. "Because of terrorist threats, there were few tourists, so I found myself virtually alone on a bus in Jerusalem with a young Palestinian tour guide. Obviously bitter, the guide decided to unload his people's problems on me. The bus turned down a side street, he pointed and said, 'that home once belonged to my family. We lived there for many years. We were thrown out and put into a refugee camp. Promises of compensation never materialized. Our family received nothing. They took our land, our homes, our businesses and even our self-respect. We have been stripped of everything and no one seems to care.'"

"For the first time," the retiring professor said, "I realized that the Jews were not the only ones being oppressed. The Palestinian people also have legitimate problems that are crying for recognition. So, I spent the last sixteen years writing articles explaining the plight of the Palestinian people and urging the necessity of looking at both sides of this difficult situation." After a long pause, the professor continued, "I must confess that in this task, I have failed completely. I worked hard to deal with a difficult worldwide problem and accomplished nothing." He then said: "I believe we are called as Christians for a special task and we will often be unsuccessful, therefore we will become depressed, and depression is the darkness that often accompanies serving God."

The retiring professor was depressed and by the time he finished speaking, we were depressed. We likely will not resolve problems between the Jews and Arabs. When we die, the world will probably be the same dangerous place it is right now. If you think about it, a little depression seems warranted. Maybe it's best to not think about it. We should do our work, raise our family, watch the news, take our vacations, enjoy a few pleasures, and not take any of this other stuff too seriously. Who am I to think that I can impact society? How much can one person do?

For generations, others asked the same question. "What can I do?" 1 John is written for a church once filled to overflowing with enthusiasm but now becoming discouraged and asking questions about their mission and even about the identity of God.

"The one who existed from the beginning is the one we have heard and seen. We saw him with our eyes and touched him with our hands. He is Jesus Christ, the Word of life. This one who is life from God was shown to us and we have seen him." (1 John 1:1-2)

John proclaims God is alive and aware of what is happening. How does he know? "We saw him and touched him." If God is alive and still in control, then our lives have purpose and meaning. We are called by God for a mission; if only we truly knew and understood what that mission was?

Next: Answers

September 13 - Answers: Following God and Dealing with Depression

1 John chapter 4

After hearing a depressed professor talk about his failure to make a difference in the Middle East, I went looking for answers and found them in the Bible through 1 John. "Dear friends, let us continue to love one another, for love comes from God." (1 John 4:7) That's it? "Love one another? Happiness is to love everybody?"

Most of us think of "love" as an intense feeling. "I love my spouse. I love to watch football. I love chocolate ice cream. I love my church." Love based on feelings makes a good romance but any marriage with too much emphasis on feelings is a one-way ticket to divorce court because feelings tend to rise and fall. People who love a church based on feelings, change churches every two or three years because feelings alone don't quite capture the meaning of love, as defined by God.

"God showed how much he loved us by sending his only Son into the world so that we might have eternal life through him. This is real love. God loved us and sent his Son as a sacrifice to take away our sins." (1 John 4:9-10) God's love goes way beyond feelings and becomes a covenant, a divine commitment, and an atoning sacrifice.

Love is an act of faith that enables the world to see God through you. Love is an attitude of grace towards those you would normally dislike. Love is a commitment to stick together when feelings are no longer enough. Love is a discipline requiring a consistent willingness to be obedient to God's will. Love is often a sacrifice, willfully putting someone else's needs before your wants. "Dear friends, since God loved us that much, we surely ought to love each other. No one has ever seen God. But if we love each other, God lives in us, and his love has been brought to full expression through us." (4:11-12) God's love is expressed through us, toward others.

But just being a loving person offers no help to the depressed professor who could not resolve the Middle East crisis. How can God call us to a mission only to experience failure? But… Did the professor really fail? In love, he offered an act of faith that enabled us to see the world with different eyes. The professor consistently wrote letters and articles about the crisis. He often sacrificed his time and energy. I left his presence profoundly changed. For me and others, his mission was a total success.

What about you? Are you seeing yourself as a failure when God has other ideas? After all, God never called us to change the world. That is His job! We are simply to be obedient by offering others the same wonderful gift of love God has given us. A word of kindness or a deed of compassion may not solve the world's problems, but it could change a life and it's the best way I know to serve God. We have no reason to be depressed or discouraged. "I write this so that you may know…" (1 John 5:13)

Prayer Challenge: God, help me to expand my definition and practice of love.

September 14 - Carl

Matthew 7:1-5

Our family flew across the United States to visit my uncle and his family in Los Angeles: home to Hollywood, Beach Boys and Disneyland. We were eagerly anticipating memorable experiences, but the best part of the whole trip was a surprise: it was the opportunity of getting to know my cousin, Carl. Carl greeted us within moments after we arrived. "Hi, cousin Larry. Would you like to see my house?" He gave us a complete tour. In the living room, Carl showed us the game table where he played with his dad. We saw the den where he watched movies and stored his wrestling magazines. But the best part of the house was his bedroom where most of his prized treasures were stored.

There were pictures and memorabilia showing Carl with various celebrities. We heard about a chance meeting with Elvis Presley and saw a photograph of the Los Angeles Dodgers baseball team signed by each player. There were albums filled with letters and pictures of family and friends. Then, Carl turned to me and asked: "Larry, why haven't you sent any pictures or letters?"

What could I say? "Carl, I didn't know how important they were to you. We'll send some family pictures when we go home. I am really sorry. Will you forgive me?"

Carl flashed the sweetest smile I've ever seen and said, "Of course, I forgive you Larry, we're family."

Carl has Down Syndrome, a genetic condition caused by the body having too many chromosomes. Symptoms include varying degrees of developmental delays. We don't know yet what causes Down Syndrome, but we do know that nearly one in every thousand babies have it. That's a lot of folks. Some would say Carl is impaired. They are wrong. Carl is different, but different is not impaired. One mother of a child with Down Syndrome wrote: "Imagine yourself to be a violet growing smack dab in the middle of a beautiful bed of daisies and the multitude of daisies surrounding you seem frustrated that you are different. They try endlessly and to the best of their abilities to turn you into a daisy, despite the fact you aren't a daisy and never will be. Is it any different with people?"

Carl is a beautiful violet surrounded by a field of daisies. Yet, I could not help but feel that Carl is one of the fortunate ones. A loving family that provides for his every need surrounds him. He is nurtured and encouraged to learn and develop at his own pace, all within a safe and wholesome environment. But one question bothered me: "Where would Carl go if anything happened to his mom and dad?"

One of the ministries I support is Heart Havens, maintaining homes for persons with disabilities who no longer have anyone to care for them. These are residential homes designed to hold three to five residents plus staff support. Virginia has more than 5,000 people on waiting lists who need this kind of support. Residents are nurtured and encouraged to develop at their own pace, all within a safe and wholesome environment.

The night before we left Los Angeles, Carl and his dad were lying on the floor in the living room watching TV. At one point, Carl scooted closer and gently put his head on dad's shoulder and whispered softly, "I love you." Together arm in arm, father and son created a magic moment that turned out to be the highlight of my vacation and a critical lesson on the meaning of "love."

Prayer Challenge: God, how can we reach out to the "Carls" all around us?

September 15 - Beverly Hillbillies Go to Church

2 Samuel chapter 6

Upon entering the sanctuary, you knew this Sunday would be different. The bulletin cover displayed the cast of "The Beverly Hillbillies." Then as you turned the page you read: "Howdy folks! Ya'll are welcome to sit a spell and hear this message of God's love. We're glad you came today and we'll be hopin' to see you right regular."

The Ringin' and Grinnin' choir was dressed hillbilly style. With an enthusiastic "yahoo ya'll," they played and sang the theme from "Davy Crockett" and "I'll Fly Away" with bells, railroad whistles and kazoos. Then, the lights dimmed, and the familiar song began, "Come and listen to a story about a man named Jed, a poor mountaineer, barely kept his family fed..." On the big screen you could see the opening of the television show. As the music faded, Jed Clampett appeared and said: "I want to thank you for invitin' me and my family to talk about God and share our faith.

Then Jethro ran in and interrupted: "Uncle Jed, can I help take up the offerin'?"

Jed Clampett responded, "Why, I reckon you can Jethro but what's an offerin'?"

Jethro replied: "An offering is when you pass the hat, and everybody fills it with money. This church uses the money to help people."

"Jethro, why can't we just give them a million dollars? No, let's make it two million so they can feed the preacher and help some poor folks too?"

Mr. Drysdale leaps from his seat and shouts: "Now see here Mr. Clampett, you can't go giving away my money, (Pauses and smiles.) I mean your money to everyone."

Jed said, "You've got a point Mr. Drysdale but we ought to give something."

"Well of course," said Mr. Drysdale. "A dollar should be enough, maybe two or you can do what I do." Mr. Drysdale smiles and then says: "You can throw your money in the air and whatever stays up, give to God. What comes down stays in my bank."

"Mr. Drysdale, that's a great idea." Jed throws up a pile of money which not only hangs in the air but forms into the shape of a cross. There is a pause while everyone stares at the floating cross of money. "Weee, doggy! I do believe we' seen a miracle," said Jed.

"I don't believe it!" Drysdale stomps off, shouting: "Miss Hathaway, where are you?"

"Jethro," said Jed Clampett. "I think the Lord has spoken." Both men solemnly remove their hats and hand them to the surprised ushers. "Let's pass the hat."

Next: Jed Clampett and Grannie Preach

September 16 – Jed Clampett and Grannie Preach

Matthew 7:7-12

Jethro opened the Bible and read: "Keep on asking, and you will be given what you ask for. Keep on looking, and you will find. Keep on knocking, and the door will be opened. For everyone who asks, receives. Everyone who seeks, finds. And the door is opened to everyone who knocks." (Mat. 7:7-8)

"That's wonderful, Jethro. But do you know what it means?" asked Jed.

"You bet I do," answered Jethro, but then he paused and admitted: "No, Uncle Jed… no, I don't know. What does it mean when it says, ask for anything and you'll get it?"

"Well, I don't rightly know myself, Jethro. What do you think, Granny?"

Granny replied: "Jed, all I know is that folks pray for food and still go hungry. These old bones of mine still ache when I get up in the morning, but I get out of that bed and cook enough fatback and hog jowls to feed all of you. Like you say, Jethro, you don't get things just by asking for them. There's a heap more to it than that."

"Weee doggie Granny, I think you're right," Jed added. "We can't get everythin' just because we ask for it. Faith in the Good Lord ain't some kind of magic wand. Faith is more a way of living during good times and bad times too. It means you respect life like it is not like what you want it to be."

"You boys come in the kitchen so I can show you something," said Granny as she walked into the kitchen and filled three pots with water and put them each on a burner. In one pot, Granny put a carrot. In another she put an egg and in the third pot she placed a handful of coffee beans. "Jethro, when you put a carrot in this pot and boil it - it gets soft. But what happens to the egg?"

"That's easy, Granny. It gets hard and I love hard-boiled eggs. Can I eat it now?"

"Settle down," said Granny.

"But Granny, what about the pot with the coffee beans?"

"That's the best part," said Granny. "Look what happens after you boil the beans."

Jethro jumped in again, "You get coffee, Granny and I love a good cup of coffee."

"Jethro, you love anything that will fit in that big mouth of yours," shouted Granny. "What I'm trying to say to you fellers is that when times get tough, some people get soft like the carrot and give up. Some folks, like the egg, look fine on the outside but inside they're hard-boiled. But coffee beans somehow turn the boiling water of trouble into a delicious fresh pot of coffee. Now Jed, that's what I call faith!"

"Granny, I believe you're right. When I look at life as a hardship it's too much. But when I look at life as a challenge it gets excitin'." Jed thought a moment and said, "It's like the words to my favorite hymn: 'Life is like a mountain railway, with an engineer that's brave. We must make the run successful, from the cradle to the grave. Watch the curves, the fills, the tunnels; never falter, never quail. Keep your hands upon the throttle and your eyes upon the rail.'" The "Beverly Hillbillies" worship service ended with everyone in the church singing: "Precious Savior, thou wilt guide us. Till we reach that blissful shore: When the angels wait to join us in Thy praise forevermore. Amen."

"Well now it's time to say goodbye to Jed and all his kin. An' they would like to thank you folks for kindly dropping in. You're all invited back again to this locality, to have a heapin' helpin' of their hospitality. Hillbilly, that is! Set a spell, Take your shoes off! Y'all come back, here!"

Prayer challenge: God help me to have faith more like the coffee bean.

September 17 - "I Don't Eat Pork!"

1 Corinthians chapter 8

Alex Haley, author of "Roots" first gained fame for writing the autobiography of Malcolm X, a famous black radical in the early 1960's. There was a story about Malcolm's change from jail-house criminal to Muslim religious leader. While in prison he received a letter from his brother talking about something new. He would send more information but, in the meantime, he wrote: "Don't smoke any cigarettes and don't eat pork."

Malcolm figured this was a scam to get out of prison. So, at the next meal as other prisoners lunged for the pork Malcolm handed his portion to the next prisoner. The prisoner asked: "Why aren't you having any pork?" Malcolm replied, "I don't eat pork!" Malcolm X referred to this incident as his conversion experience. When he said, "I don't eat pork!" he took a first step toward God. Malcolm then said: "If you take one step toward God. God will take two steps toward you."

As sincere and committed Christians we too must be prepared to stand up and say to the world, "I don't eat pork!" Our priorities change. We claim to love the Lord with all our heart, with all our soul and with all our mind. We say we love others as much as we do ourselves. So, we should act differently, and think differently, shouldn't we? This noticeable change in attitude becomes our witness to the outside world.

A family met for lunch after church and spent the entire meal criticizing their pastor and church. One woman was concerned but didn't know what to say? She tried being quiet. She tried making positive statements. Nothing worked. "Maybe I should just tell them off, get up from the table and leave!" she said. "But they're my family. I love them. What should I do?" Several weeks later, she said, "The Lord answered my prayers. During lunch when the conversation began to sour, I suggested we say a prayer for our pastor and church. There was a long silence, but my uncle said, 'I think it's a great idea,' and next thing I knew we were praying together and afterward, the criticism stopped."

Every day, God gives you a chance to say to the world, "I don't eat pork." In other words: If you were arrested for being a Christian, would they have enough evidence to convict you? Paul goes on to say, "Anyone who claims to know all the answers doesn't really know very much. But the person who loves God is the one God knows and cares for." (1 Cor. 8:2-3) Actions speak louder than words.

One reader wrote: "My boyfriend came to church with me. After the service, he went home and wrote that he was touched by what you said. He always felt misjudged in church, but it wasn't like that for him this time. He knew he needed to thank God for the good in his life and for allowing the two of us to be together. However, it took going to church for him to realize it. I want to thank you because that Sunday, he took one step toward God, but God took three steps toward him."

Prayer Challenge: Lord, help me strengthen my witness to the world around me.

September 18 - Moses and Failure

Exodus chapter 2

Enthusiasm can be misleading. We are tempted to promote the victory of Christianity without warning of the cost. "Become a Christian and live happily ever after," we too quickly say but fail to explain what ever after means. Readers Digest told of two seminary students who went door-to-door sharing their faith. At one house the students walked through a gauntlet of screaming children and barking dogs. A tired mother opened the door. "We would like to tell you how to obtain eternal life," they proclaimed. She hesitated, then looked at the yard full of toys, at her house full of children and softly sighed before replying, "Thank you, but no thanks. I couldn't stand it!"

Becoming a Christian is no guarantee you will live happily ever after. There are times of defeat and failure. We let down our family, our church and we even let down God. In the Bible, experiencing failure is often when God teaches unforgettable lessons. How about Moses? Moses was God's man who rescued his people from Pharaoh, parted the Red Sea and received the Ten Commandments. As a baby, he was raised by Pharaoh's daughter with the best education available.

For the first forty years of his life, Moses literally had it made.

"Moses saw how hard the Israelites were forced to work. He saw an Egyptian beating one of the Hebrew slaves. After looking around to make sure no one was watching, Moses killed the Egyptian and buried him in the sand." (Ex 2:11-12) Thinking he had won respect, Moses was shocked to find he was scorned and in a matter of days, forced to flee for his life. For the next forty years, Moses would hide out in the desert as a lowly shepherd. Where did Moses go wrong? He committed murder. You don't cheat on your taxes and then give a portion to God. Moses did it his way not God's way. Spiritual leadership only comes from God so you can never just reach out and grab it. Burying your mistakes in the sand never erases them; it only postpones the discovery.

Moses spent forty years in the desert wondering what might have been. Wait! This would all be depressing if we didn't know how it ended. At the tender age of eighty, God called Moses from a burning bush to lead the Hebrews out of Egypt. This time Moses was ready to listen and rely upon God and the rest is history. Yes, the life of a Christian promises exciting times on the mountaintop and it also promises painful lessons learned only in the desert. Maybe you've been there recently and you're feeling the pain. God has not forgotten you. Whether you are eight or eighty, God is never absent.

Andre Crouch wrote: "I've had many tears and sorrows. I've had questions for tomorrow. There've been times I didn't know right from wrong! But in every situation, God gave blessed consolation that my trials come to only make me strong. Through it all; through it all; I've learned to trust in Jesus. I've learned to trust in God. Through it all; through it all; I've learned to depend upon God's word."

Prayer Challenge: God, help me learn from my mistakes and grow stronger.

September 19 - 1953

Luke 5:36-39

I was born in 1953. On a whim, I did a little googling to find out what it was like to live then. As Americans, we were scared; Communism seemed to be taking over the world: The Korean War was ending but Korea remained divided. The Soviet Union detonated a hydrogen bomb. School children practiced, "Duck and Cover" in case of nuclear attack. Bomb shelters were built in backyards. Senator McCarthy exposed communists. Julius and Ethel Rosenberg were executed for selling secrets to the atomic bomb. Leonard Bernstein, Lena Horn, Orson Wells, Arthur Miller are among those black-listed.

In 1953 President Eisenhower is inaugurated on live TV but twice as many people watch "Lucy" give birth the night before. Automobiles flourish and an interstate road system begins construction. Segregation is still a grim reality. The "Baby Boom" is in full force as our economy thrives on consumer goods. Since 1953, technology has added digital televisions, VCR's, cell phones, computers, the internet, and microwave ovens. Yet with all the improvements, many of us work longer hours, face more stress, have more disposable income yet have less free time and energy to enjoy it.

The innocence of the "fifties" was replaced by the cynicism of the 21st Century. Trust in government, institutions, churches and almost any large organization is at an all-time low. Family structures which usually meant mom, dad and two to three kids now are best described as... "complicated!"

Since 1953, a lot has changed. But what about the church? In those years of change and turmoil, what happened to the church? One reader responded: "I realized the church has easily been the worst part of my life: The institutional church that is. What should have been an oasis has been a desert. A preacher asked: Can God spread a table in the desert? He surely can and does. My feast has been first God and then friends, especially Christians. I realized with some relief that it's the people, not the institution that is the church. New wine will burst the old wineskin if not replaced but people keep hanging onto the old wineskin."

"What should have been an oasis has been a desert." Is this an isolated opinion or do others agree? Recent surveys show most Americans believe in God, but that percentage goes way down when asked about the church. Amid years filled with change and turmoil many search for something to believe.

Next: How can the church better respond to our rapidly changing world?

September 20 - 1953 Change, and The Church

1 Peter chapter 1

Since 1953, there have been technological shifts with the result that we can do almost anything faster and more efficiently. In theory this allows more time for family and friends and offers opportunities for contentment and happiness, but the reality is quite a different story. Instead, stress related disorders are at an all-time high and families are more dysfunctional than ever. During those same years, church attendance and participation dramatically declined. One reader bluntly stated: "What should have been an oasis has been a desert."

Another reader wrote: "A few years ago, I went through a divorce. A member of my Sunday school class verbally condemned me. I quit attending Sunday school. I came to church broken and often in despair. The people didn't notice the pain in my eyes or the brokenness in my heart. I came to church less and less frequently."

But one reader offered a very different perspective: "I walked into a church to see a play my son was in. I had not set foot inside for several years. In fact, I had given up on Christianity. Something melted inside my heart.

I felt an aching sense that I was missing something which could fill the spiritual hole inside me. The pull of that service kept tugging on me and I kept going back. The church has been responsible for nurturing my spiritual growth through services, Bible Studies, workshops, prayer - the list goes on. Why is church important to me? Without it, I would still be lost."

The Apostle Peter offered this advice: "So think clearly and exercise self-control. Look forward to the special blessings that will come to you at the return of Jesus Christ. Obey God because you are his children. Don't slip back into your old ways of doing evil; you didn't know any better then. But now you must be holy in everything you do, just as God—who chose you to be his children—is holy. For he himself has said, 'You must be holy because I am holy.'" (1 Peter 1:13-16)

Peter is fervently reminding the church: During times of chaos the church should think clearly and exercise self-control. Surrounded by cynicism, the church looks forward to special blessings. The world promotes, "anything goes philosophy" but we, "obey God because we are His children." The church keeps us from slipping back into our old ways of doing evil. The church helps us to be holy in everything we do.

Many churches struggle to find meaning and simply survive but others grow stronger and are blessed. Why? What lessons can we learn? In Hebrews: "And so, dear brothers and sisters, we can boldly enter heaven's

Most Holy Place because of the blood of Jesus. This is the new, life-giving way that Christ has opened for us through the sacred curtain, by means of his death for us." (Hebrews 10:19-20)

Next: After Years of turmoil and disruptive change, action steps for the church.

September 21 - Church Response to 1953

Hebrews chapter 10

God makes an extraordinary promise to the church: "We can boldly enter heaven's Most Holy Place because of the blood of Jesus." (Hebrews 10:19) What does that mean? First, we must prepare and nurture our faith.

Ten Foundation Words help a church stay focused on God: **Pray:** One prayer group met just to pray "that our church would continue hearing God's voice." **Listen:** God's voice is quiet and can come from anywhere, anytime and from anyone. **Bible:** Everything should be designed around being guided by God's Authoritative Word. **Worship:** More than music or sermon: Worship should enable you to feel God's presence. **Fellowship:** Covered-dish suppers or youth gatherings: fellowship strengthens relationships. **Growth:** Is your walk with God growing stronger? What are you doing to nurture your faith? **Grace:** As family, God's grace is a reminder we may stumble but help is there to give us a lift. **Witness:** God's amazing gift of grace is meant to be freely shared with friends and strangers. **Ministry:** God's love at work within you for good deeds, whether in church or community. **Mission:** Reaching beyond your church walls with acts of love and charity for those in need.

"And since we have a great High Priest who rules over God's people, let us go right into the presence of God, with true hearts fully trusting him. For our evil consciences have been sprinkled with Christ's blood to make us clean, and our bodies have been washed with pure water." (21-22) Once again we are encouraged to trust and be bold so here are ten action words any church should consider if they want to boldly serve God and make a difference in their community and our world.

Ten Action Words for a bold church: **Risk-taking:** God often calls on a church to take great risks before seeing great miracles. **Best:** Every church should strive to be the best at something according to their talents. **Passion:** Do you get excited when you talk about what's happening at your church? **Creative:** The joke around our church is that you never know what will happen next. **Alert:** Opportunities often come where you least expect them. **Open:** Sometimes the best ideas come from people who are not a regular part of your church. **Basic:** Never forget our basic task is helping each other serve and love God. **Relevant:** How can what we see and hear Sunday help us become better Christians Monday? **Encourage:** How can we encourage one another to outbursts of love and good deeds? **Comfort:** God is a God of comfort who will see us through so we can then comfort others.

If we do this, God will be with us: "Without wavering, let us hold tightly to the hope we say we have, for God can be trusted to keep his promise. Think of ways to encourage one another to outbursts of love and good deeds. And let us not neglect our meeting together, as some people do, but encourage and warn each other, especially now that the day of his coming back again is drawing near." (23-25) Over the years, much has changed but those years serve as a vivid reminder our need for God's church is stronger than ever. We must be bold proclaiming God's Word to the world.

Next: Examples and Letters

September 22 - Letters

1 Peter chapter 2

"A few weeks ago, I asked for prayer about attending church, after a long desert journey wandering away. I have been visiting a wonderful church since my last email and have signed up for ministries and classes to strengthen my walk."

"Often the church is referred to as light. Like a moth, I am drawn to the light. Sometimes I fly close to the light and enjoy the warmth. Other times I stray into the dimly lit area and fly my own way. God allows me to dart out into the dark, but I am always drawn back to the light of the church."

"Some of our children moved away but when they visit, they always want to go to our church because this is home. Having lost my husband, this church was my salvation. I cannot imagine being anywhere other than here. This is my home and my family."

"Outside the Church doors, there are so many distractions and people who are different in their interests, beliefs, values, priorities. Inside is a safe haven, a place to commune, worship, and learn. I thank God we have the privilege and freedom of going to Church."

"My church planted important seeds in my life. My church is an anchor when winds howl, storms come, and turbulent seas become too rough. As I head toward the Lords Day, I can see a lighthouse guiding me and an anchor that holds me fast. When I step through those church doors, I feel peaceful and realize I was never alone in the storm: One greater than I was there all along."

"We had a youth group called 'The Way Station' which met every Friday night to hear Gods word, share testimonies, and sing songs. My Christian life grew so much during that time. I often wonder if I would be a Christian today without that experience."

"I am a retired Marine. The church is important to me because in the twenty years I served our country, traveling around the world; it became my family. No matter where I went, my family was there waiting."

"I was a Youth Pastor when my marriage fell apart. I stepped down. I couldn't serve God effectively and go through the pain. I pulled away from God and everyone around me. I fell into a deep depression and reached the point that I couldn't see any reason to continue living. It was my relationship with God and the church family praying for me that pulled me out of the depression. I now lead a divorce care group."

How has the church been an important part of your life? Despite the many problems and shortcomings, the church is still the best place I know to strengthen your connection with Christ and find your God-given purpose for living.

Prayer Challenge: May God inspire our response to the needs around us.

September 23 - Stress Disease

1 Corinthians chapter 12

I don't mean to complain but the last few weeks have been stressful. There are staff changes and new employees to train. People are visiting and I can't find time to meet them. Several church members have experienced tragedies, and I must be there for them. My church has a bigger budget. My dog's medicine keeps her awake all night and she's driving me crazy. My computer is in the shop.

Moan and groan! Have you noticed the emphasis on me? Everything is about me! Stress is closely related to the dreaded disease known as: ME, MYSELF, AND I. You're afflicted when you say: "I must do everything myself if it's to be done right! You just can't find good help! No one ever volunteers but me!" Are you catching on? The "me, myself and I" disease infects most of us occasionally but if you don't seek treatment, you will suffer immeasurable pain and lose a few friends.

Fortunately, God has a prescription: quiet reflection, a measure of prayer and a solid dose of Bible study. "Now there are different kinds of spiritual gifts, but it is the same Holy Spirit who is the source of them all. There are different kinds of service in the church, but it is the same Lord we are serving. There are different ways God works in our lives, but it is the same God who does the work through all of us. A spiritual gift is given to each of us as a means of helping the entire church. (1 Corinthians 12:4-7)

The common interpretation of this passage is, "All of us are different with various talents and abilities." But recently I noticed another lesson. Look at the second part of each sentence: different kinds of spiritual gifts, but the same Holy Spirit. Different kinds of service but the same Lord. Different ways God works but the same God.

The emphasis was never meant to be on our gifts, however good. Three times the author makes the point: "the same Holy Spirit, the same Lord and the same God." In other words, we all have different gifts, but we are all coordinated and encouraged by the same Lord. It is God who is ultimately in control, not me. When I put the emphasis on me, myself, and I the result is always the same: chaos and stress. But with God in control there is always another way.

Look at my complaints again: Staff changes. Every staff change resulted in needed help. People visit our church. And this is a problem? Church members experienced tragedies. Yet during those tragedies, I found God giving comfort. Our church has a bigger budget. Each time the budget grows we are touching another life for God. My dog's medicine keeps her awake. But the medicine is keeping her alive and I'm thankful. My computer is in the shop. Could this be God's way of providing time for prayer?

Paul promised: "A spiritual gift is given to each of us as a means of helping the entire church." Our church functions better and my stress level goes down when I learn to stop thinking everything revolves around me and trust God to provide the people and resources we need. "Lord, please replace my stress with faith in You!" Now, if God would only help my dog sleep all night.

Prayer Challenge: Lord, help me to replace poor me with faith and trust in You.

September 24 - Success

1 Corinthians 1

How would you define success? Must you be rich? Own your company? Become famous? Does it include world travel? Extensive education? Becoming the best in your field? Does success mean happiness, good health, and a sexy body? I once attended a "Success Seminar" and for eleven hours, I listened to ten of the best speakers in the world share their definitions of success.

A politician talked about how old-fashioned values still succeed in the modern world. A motivational speaker spoke of the importance of relationships: business relationships, family relationships and especially our relationship with God. A TV personality shared his personal struggles while coping with the murder of his son to show how we can turn tragedy into triumph. A doctor helped us understand how proper eating habits and exercise can tune our bodies and minds into more productive tools. An author showed how goal setting could transform our lives. Another speaker spoke of levels of success and how we often keep ourselves trapped at a lower level.

Christopher Reeve, the actor and advocate for victims of spinal cord injury made a comment that defines success for me. "Success means letting the relationships in your life grow and transcend into the highest possible levels. It also means not putting yourself first in life and remembering that the more you give away, the more you have." Reeve earned the right to cry: "I'm a victim." Yet he chose to do the best he could with what he had by concentrating on two essential ingredients of success:

One: Letting relationships transcend into the highest levels calls for a willingness to shift your priorities. Two: Not putting yourself first and remembering that the more you give away, the more you have. Putting others first is not a sign of weakness, but an indicator of vast strength. Success means learning to give. Paul wrote: "I can never stop thanking God for the generous gifts he has given you. He has enriched your church with the gifts of eloquence and every kind of knowledge. This shows that what I told you about Christ is true. Now you have every spiritual gift you need as you eagerly wait for the return of our Lord. He will keep you strong right up to the end." (1 Cor. 1:4-8)

Success means thanking God for the gifts given to you. Success means knowing you belong to Christ. Success is understanding that you have been enriched with gifts and knowledge. Success means using those gifts as you eagerly wait for Christ's return. Success means relying on God to keep you strong right up to the end.

Are you looking for that elusive obsession called success? First, discover what success means and then be willing to work for it with every talent you possess. Paul wrote: "Be strong and steady, always enthusiastic about the Lord's work, for you know that nothing you do for the Lord is ever useless." (1 Corinthians 15:58)

Prayer Challenge: Lord, help me work toward success in Your Eyes.

September 25 - Make A Difference?

2 Corinthians chapter 5

Quiz: Name the ten wealthiest people. Name the last ten Super Bowl winners. How about the last ten Academy Award winning movies? The last five Nobel Prize winners? No? I didn't do well either. Apart from a few trivia nuts, few of us remember past achievements. If you want to make a difference? Accomplishments is not the answer.

To make a difference you need to look beyond achievements. God has something else in mind. Paul says: "That is why we live by believing and not by seeing." (2 Cor. 5:7) If we live by believing, then we must look past achievements. The answer? "So, our aim is to please him always." (v9) We concentrate our creative energy in pleasing God.

Pleasing God is a good goal but how?" Paul answers in verse 11, "It is because we know this solemn fear of the Lord that we try to work so hard to persuade others." The word "fear" in this case refers more to loving respect than terror. So, if we want to make a difference, Paul provides two steps to follow: Work on developing our relationship with God and try to influence others.

Let's look at another quiz. See how you do on this one: Think of three people you enjoy spending time with. Name 5 friends who helped you through a difficult time. List two churches that made a difference in someone's life. List three teachers who influenced your education. Easier? It was for me, too.

Making a difference can mean many things for many people: Justine felt called to lead the youth in ministry. Betsy felt the call to help hundreds discover their spiritual gifts. Fay visits shut-ins and works with older adults. Jim leads an organization that repairs run-down houses for the elderly and poor. Frank and his crew do construction chores for other churches and people in need.

Do you still want to make a difference? Work to improve your personal relationship with God. Join a Bible Study and spend time in prayer. Look around and ask God to help you see more clearly those who are hurting. Look for ways to actively help where you see a need. Say something encouraging to at least one person daily. When someone asks you for prayer, pray with them!

Remember, you are called to be involved in your church, your community, and your world. This isn't everything, but it's a good start. We can work to make a difference with friends, family, fellow employees, our local church, our community, and our needy world! What a relief. I can't even remember this year's super bowl winner.

Prayer Challenge: God, help me make a difference for someone today.

September 26 - Computer Crash

Romans chapter 12

My computer crashed and died and erased most of my cell phone data on the same day an infamous email virus struck throughout the world. Critical files were in danger of being lost. So, I reacted like any technologically handicapped person and panicked. I grabbed my precious cargo and raced to the local computer doctor pleading for help. "Shoot me straight, Doc. I can take it! Is it the love bug?"

He smiled and looked at me for the longest time. (I hate it when they do that!) After a lecture on the importance of backing up files and avoiding unnecessary downloads the doctor prescribed five days of bed rest and therapy (for my devices).

Five days! What would I do without my devices for five days? There was important work to do! It was at this point I realized there was a problem but not with my computer! The Apostle Paul gives this warning: "Don't copy the behavior and customs of this world, but let God transform you into a new person by changing the way you think. Then you will know what God wants you to do and you will know how good and pleasing his will really is." (Romans 12:2)

As a follower of God, I was caught up in the day-by-day demands and customs of this world, namely my phone and computer, so I needed to change the way I think. In other words, I was doing the work, but I was neglecting something far more valuable: my intimate relationship with God.

What about you? What are your priorities? Most likely your priorities are whatever saps much of your time and energy. Could it be the pressure to succeed in a highly competitive work environment? Maybe you're feeling the daily grind of maintaining a household and caring for children. Are you caught up in the mind-numbing allure of any number of entertainment pleasures?

My first day without communication devices was taxing. Like any addict, I needed a computer fix. "How do I write my devotion? Where is my schedule? What if I borrowed somebody else's computer? Maybe, I'll buy a new one." The hours dragged on and on. I was feeling lost and vulnerable, right where God wanted me.

Something happened during those forced periods of solitude. I did more reading and a lot more praying. During a forced withdrawal from my hectic routine, I discovered a gem of Biblical truth.

Next: Computer Crash and Four Prescriptions.

September 27 - Computer Crash & Four Prescriptions

Proverbs 1:23-27

After my computer crashed the doctor prescribed five days of bed rest and therapy (for my devices). "Five days!" I thought. "What would I do for five days? There was important work to do!" It was at this point I realized there was a problem but not with the computer! My devices were sapping my creative energy and stealing my time and preventing me from becoming all God planned. My priorities were out of order.

The first day was tough. The hours seemed to drag on and on. I was feeling lost and vulnerable, obviously where God wanted me. "Maybe I should read? Yes, read!" I picked up a story about a doctor giving advice to someone going through a desolate period in life. The doctor said: "Find an isolated area, leave your phone behind and take one of these four prescriptions every three hours." There were four prescriptions. The first contained only two words: "1) Listen carefully."

Listen carefully? Listen to what? My telephone and computer are in the shop. This was going to be more difficult than I thought. At first, I could only pace the room and fret, but slowly, ever so slowly, I began to settle down. Finally, something inside me seemed to whisper, "Read Proverbs." The first chapter of Proverbs hit me like a bowling ball rolling toward a perfect strike. "Come here and listen to me! I'll pour out the spirit of wisdom upon you and make you wise." (1:23) God wasn't impressed with my productivity, my writing, or my ministry. Like a wise parent, God urged me to sit still and listen, really listen. Lately, I've been too busy. Imagine that and I'm a preacher! What about you?

As the hours passed, I began to relax. Reading turned to thinking and thinking led naturally to prayer. No longer in a hurry, I freely and openly shared frustrations and personal concerns. Then I began to listen for the comforting voice of God. Inevitably, there would be a gentle nudge to read Scripture or write a note. As the hours passed, I learned that being quiet and taking the time to listen is seldom a time waster. It's excellent preparation. I learned that it's difficult to really understand someone until you first make time to listen to what they say. I learned that it's impossible to hear the sweet, soft voice of God until you slow your frantic pace and listen.

Are you feeling the pressure? Slowing down, becoming aware of your surroundings, listening to coworkers, and listening to God's still, quiet voice will calm your nerves and help you discover new insights. New insights become keys to spiritual growth. Are you feeling the daily grind of raising a family? Taking the initiative to slow down and listen could even help you understand your crazy teenager. (Nahh!! But it may give you more patience.) Are you watching too much TV? Spending too much time on Facebook? Maybe you're substituting entertainment for much-needed quiet and contemplation time. "Listen carefully" was advice I needed to follow. Maybe you need it too.

Next: Prescription #2. Meanwhile, "Listen Carefully."

September 28 - Prescription #2

Hebrews chapter 11, Proverbs 6:20-23

"Five days with no communication device! What would I do?" I had a problem, but it wasn't the computer. An article provided four prescriptions for overcoming bleak periods. The first prescription was "Listen carefully." Did you try it?

As the hours passed, I slowly began to relax. Listening soon led to prayer and prayer led to a quiet stillness and the comforting presence of God. At times, there would be prompting to read a particular scripture or write a brief note. "Listen carefully" was a reminder that even in this fast-paced environment, God is still very much in control. By now I was ready to open the doctor's second prescription: "Try reaching back."

"Try reaching back? For what?" On my desk was a photo album containing a few of my favorite pictures. "Memories? Is that what I'm supposed to reach back for?" I flipped the pages of the album slowly and began to sort through each priceless photograph. Each picture took on a life of its own reminding me of the story behind the image. There were: Baby pictures. "My how they have grown." Loving moments with Mell, my wife. "We don't do this nearly often enough!" Family vacations and parties. "Was I really that crazy?" Special ministry moments. "Priceless!" Pets and their antics. "Our dogs always seemed to brighten our day."

Each picture represented a new story to remember and enjoy. Each story revealed golden moments to savor and appreciate. Each golden moment became a treasure trove of memories offering reassurance that I am a precious child of God, created for a purpose and that purpose is realized in the faces and the hearts of those I have had the privilege to love and receive love in return.

At first, I didn't expect much help from the Bible because there are no photographs. I was so wrong! Each chapter contains God's valuable word pictures imploring us to learn and remember. Genealogy lists serve as vivid reminders of those people who went before us. Stories illustrate the struggles of real people valiantly striving to serve God. Poetry praising God or crying out for help during crisis. Jesus' reminder to, "eat this bread and drink this wine in remembrance of me." Hebrews illustrating heroes of our faith. Paul's letters reminding us of God's grace.

"My son, obey your father's commands and don't neglect your mother's teaching. Keep their words always in your heart. Wherever you walk, their counsel can lead you." (Proverbs 6:20-22) Reaching back helps you recall the teaching of God and your family. Reaching back offers reassurance that your life has meaning and a purpose. Reaching back can be the spark that rekindles your fire. Reaching back is the reminder you are never alone. Reach back into your own album of precious memories. I pray you receive a spark to rekindle your fire.

Next: Prescription 3. I feel better today. Thank you, God.

September 29 - Prescription #3

Proverbs chapter 8

The computer was in the shop, but I was the one in need of help. While searching for answers, I ran across a doctor's advice: "Find an isolated spot and follow the instructions on four separate slips of paper." While reading the four prescriptions I also studied the book of Proverbs. The combination proved invaluable.

Listen Carefully was a reminder that in this fast-paced world, God is still in control. I was the one who needed to pause. "Come here and listen to me! I'll pour out the spirit of wisdom upon you and make you wise." (Proverbs 1:23)

Try Reaching Back. A photo album represented precious memories and golden moments. Each moment became a treasure trove of memories offering reassurance that I am loved and shaped by God, family, and friends. "Wherever you walk, their counsel can lead you. When you sleep, they will protect you." (Proverbs 6:22)

So far, so good! I was eagerly anticipating opening the third prescription. Carefully unfolding the third piece of paper, I read: "Reexamine Your Motives." What? Reexamine your motives? Why? I work hard to be successful and provide for my family. I enjoy being good at what I do. Is there anything wrong with that?

A quiet authoritative voice seemed to whisper: "Maybe. It all depends on what you're working for. What are your real motives?" Truthfully, my motives had subtly changed. I enjoyed the adulation and compliments success can bring. I yearned to be recognized as an authority among my colleagues. I liked having a little extra money in my checkbook. Is it wrong to desire the fruit of my creative labors?

Notice the emphasis on "I" and "my"? In other words: "I" had a problem. Reexamine your motives means: Are you working for something bigger than yourself? "Choose God's instruction rather than silver and knowledge over pure gold. For wisdom is far more valuable than rubies. Nothing you desire can be compared with it." (8:10-11)

I thought this was a reminder to spend time in Bible study. Yes, but God is also showing us where to focus our motives. Silver and gold are the motives of personal status and financial security. Instruction and wisdom represent striving for something beyond personal accomplishments. God promises: "Nothing you desire can be compared with it."

Reexamine your motives is a call to discover God's purpose for your life and carry it out. Reexamine your motives provides the comfort of knowing you are valued for who you are. Reexamine your motives requires courage to reach beyond what is comfortable. Reexamine your motives demands humility because ultimate success belongs to God. Reexamine your motives promises gifts far greater than anything you've ever imagined.

"Reexamine your motives" was a message from God for me to repent. "Forgive me Lord. Purify my heart and help me change." In the quiet of the early morning hours, alone in my study, I began to cry. Embarrassed, I tried to wipe away the tears, but they would not stop. For several minutes, I was trapped by an overwhelming sense of guilt. Yet, this is exactly where God wanted me. Because without discovering a need to change, I would never understand what happened next.

Next: "Reexamine your motives" is a call from God to repent. Now what?

September 30 - Prescription #4

Proverbs 8:32-36

It took five days without my communication devices to teach me that I was the one who really needed fixing. While doing some serious soul-searching, I read a doctor's advice for overcoming difficulties. "Find an isolated spot and follow the instructions on four slips of paper." So, I settled down one long night to study each of the four prescriptions along with the book of Proverbs.

1. **Listen Carefully.** A poignant reminder that in this fast-paced world, God is still in control. I was the one who needed help. "Come and listen to me! I'll pour out the spirit of wisdom upon you and make you wise." (Proverbs 1:23)
2. **Try Reaching Back.** A photo album provided precious memories and golden moments to savor and appreciate. A treasure trove offering reassurance of the love and acceptance of God, family and friends. "Wherever you walk, their counsel can lead you. When you sleep, they will protect you." (Proverbs 6:22)
3. **Reexamine Your Motives.** Are you working for something bigger than yourself? Whether it's a call to discover God's purpose for my life or the comfort of knowing that I am valued for who I am, I needed to reexamine my motives.

> "Those who search for me will surely find me." (Proverbs 8:17)

I needed to change to fully understand what would happen next: The fourth prescription. Carefully, I opened the piece of paper and studied the six words: Write your troubles in the sand. For a long time, I didn't know how to respond. The idea of standing on a quiet beach writing my troubles in the sand and seeing them washed away by the incoming tide was certainly comforting.

Could it be that simple? No! There is something missing. Troubles don't disappear so easily. Melancholy is not so quickly washed away. Then I read this passage from Proverbs: "Happy are those who listen to me, watching for me daily at my gates, waiting for me outside my home! For whoever finds me, finds life." (8:34-35)

"Listen to Me. Watch for Me. Wait for Me. If you find Me, you find life." This verse turned out to be the answer, but I didn't realize it until I noticed a painting by Thomas Kinkade entitled "A Lighthouse in the Storm." At first, all you see in the painting are waves crashing against the beach poised to destroy all within their path. It would be a bleak picture if not for the lighthouse. The bright light shining in the storm looks reassuring, comforting. You sense that no matter how hard the storm rages, the lighthouse will continue to stand and provide a light to guide the lost.

Write your troubles in the sand, can only take us so far. The foaming waves still attack the beach. Where will I look to receive strength? The fierce winds still blow you off course. Where will you find a steady light to guide your way? We need a lighthouse to provide direction and stability. God says: Listen to Me. Watch for Me. Wait for Me. If you find Me? You find life. So, the four prescriptions combined with God's message from proverbs provided a framework I continue to rely on today:

1. **Listen carefully**. God is in control. "Come here and listen to me."
2. **Try reaching back**. Look for your treasure trove of memories to guide you."
3. **Reexamine your motives**. "Those who search for me will find me."
4. **Write your troubles in the sand**. "If you find me, you find life."

Finally, I added: **Look to the lighthouse**. God's steady light to guide your way. "If you find me, you find life." As the early morning rays slowly crossed the horizon, I realized it had been a long but satisfying night. I lost a computer and a phone for a few days, but I gained something far more precious: a restored and renewed relationship with my precious Lord. "Your Word is a lamp for my feet, a light for my path." (Psalm 119:105)

Prayer Challenge: Try applying the four prescriptions as you read more of Proverbs.

Don't miss out on continuing the daily devotions. Order Book 4: Fall "A Daily Dose of Godly Encouragement: Medicine for Tough Days."

While ordering, don't forget to leave a review. Your review can help people who have never read these daily devotions consider ordering a book and strengthening their faith in God.

More from Larry Davies

Don't miss the next book available soon on Amazon.com:

Book 4: Fall to Christmas
A Daily Dose of Godly Encouragement:
Medicine for Tough Days.

Other Books by Larry Davies

A Daily Dose of Godly Encouragement: Medicine for Tough Days
Book 1: Winter
Book 2: Spring
Book 3: Summer

Live the Light:
Five Weeks to a Life that Shines

Breaking the Peanut Butter Habit:
Following God's Recipe for a Better Life

When A Used Car Salsman Becomes A Preacher…
There Must Be A God!

Sowing Seeds of Faith:
In A World Gone Bonkers!

A Daily Dose of Godly Encouragement: Medicine for Tough Days

Message Series from Larry on YouTube:
SowingSeedsofFaith.com/Sermons

"Prayer – Care – Share"
"Live the L.I.G.H.T."
"Now What?!"
"It's Not Your Birthday!"
"What Does It Mean to be United Methodist?"
"Luke and Jesus"
"Acts: The Church Begins"